COUNT
THE
RINGS!

COUNT
THE
RINGS!

Inside **Boston's Wicked Awesome** Reign
as the City of Champions

FROM 2001 TO 2017, TEN TITLES, FOUR TEAMS
RED SOX, PATRIOTS, BRUINS, AND CELTICS

BOB HALLORAN

Guilford, Connecticut

An imprint of Globe Pequot

Distributed by NATIONAL BOOK NETWORK

British Library Cataloguing in Publication Information available

Library of Congress Cataloging-in-Publication Data available

ISBN 978-1-4930-3008-8 (hardcover)
ISBN 978-1-4930-3009-5 (e-book)

∞™ The paper used in this publication meets the minimum requirements of American National Standard for Information Sciences—Permanence of Paper for Printed Library Materials, ANSI/NISO Z39.48-1992.

Printed in the United States of America

ACKNOWLEDGMENTS

I think the concept of *Count The Rings* is a sensational idea, and I can say that without bragging, because it wasn't my idea. So, special thanks to Keith Wallman for envisioning this book and offering me the opportunity to execute it. The layout of the book, which has been called by some a "bookazine", because of its similarities to a magazine, is also the brainchild of Keith and his staff. They're very good at what they do.

And it couldn't have been easy for Rick Rinehart to take over the reins of this project midway through it, but he did so seamlessly and brought it home. Thanks, Rick.

I don't know how Albert Dickson found so many great photos, but I'm glad he did, and I appreciate him writing the captions.

And let's go with "Wow"! Robert Kraft wrote the foreword! That was huge, and I can't thank him enough. The process started with Keith asking, "Do you think there's any way you could get Mr. Kraft to write the foreword? He's at the top of our wish list."

"Well," I said, "there's definitely a chance." I went directly to Stacey James, the Patriots Vice President of Media Relations, all-around good guy, and Robert Kraft's right hand man. Stacey put in the ask, and Mr. Kraft said yes, telling me later, "It's because you're a gentleman." I thank him for that and for his sentiments that begin this book. And of course, thank you, Stacey!

My manager, Matt Valentinas, always gets a big thank-you for his unyielding support and readiness to take care of everything that I don't have the time, talent, or intelligence to.

And special thanks to my other manager, my wife, Eileen Curran, who understands that when I'm working a full-time job and writing a book, that a lot of household responsibilities may not get done in a timely fashion. At least, I think she understands. Let me ask her. Nope, she still wants the lawn mowed in a timely fashion. Love you, honey!

Thanks to my children, Sean, Dan, Liam, and Grace, who didn't do much relative to this book, but when else are they going to get their names in a book? I love you all!

And how about this? To all New England sports fans, thank you for your passion! You make being a sports reporter in Boston exciting, challenging, and relevant. You didn't really have anything to do with writing this book, but if it weren't for you, believe me, this book would never have been written. So, thank you! I hope you enjoyed the walk down memory lane. And I hope for your sake that we add a few more chapters real soon.

➤ CONTENTS

Foreword by Robert Kraft 2

Introduction. 6

CHAPTER ONE: **THE 2001 NEW ENGLAND PATRIOTS** 10

CHAPTER TWO: **THE 2003 NEW ENGLAND PATRIOTS** 22

CHAPTER THREE: **THE 2004 BOSTON RED SOX** 36

CHAPTER FOUR: **THE 2004 NEW ENGLAND PATRIOTS** 62

CHAPTER FIVE: **THE 2007 BOSTON RED SOX** 82

CHAPTER SIX: **THE 2007–08 BOSTON CELTICS** 104

CHAPTER SEVEN: **THE 2010–11 BOSTON BRUINS** 126

CHAPTER EIGHT: **THE 2013 BOSTON RED SOX** 146

CHAPTER NINE: **THE 2014 NEW ENGLAND PATRIOTS** 170

CHAPTER TEN: **THE 2016 NEW ENGLAND PATRIOTS** 196

About the Author 218

People forget. Throughout the 1990s, Boston sports fans were generally miserable. Then 2001 happened.

While Patriots fans will always remember how that incredible season ended, we often forget the chilling details of how it began and the anguish that Boston sports fans were feeling at the time. In 2001, New England was experiencing a championship drought. The Celtics had gone 15 years since last winning a title in 1986. The Bruins hadn't won the Stanley Cup in nearly 30 years (since 1972). The Patriots had gone to the Super Bowl twice in our 41-year history, but lost both times. And the Red Sox hadn't won a World Series since Babe Ruth pitched for Boston in 1918 – 83 years earlier. By 2001, Boston sports talk radio had dubbed its New England audiences the "fellowship of the miserable."

Our younger fans simply can't imagine what it was like . . . and I hope they never will.

For the Patriots, the 2001 season began with some devastating losses, both on and off the field. Our quarterbacks coach, Dick Rehbein, unexpectedly collapsed and died during training camp. A few weeks later, we lost our number one wide receiver, Terry Glenn, who left camp and ultimately returned, but only appeared in four games all season. Two days after losing the season opener at Cincinnati, we suffered one of our greatest losses as a nation with the tragic events of 9/11. The NFL suspended operations to mourn with the rest of America. When the season resumed, the Patriots suffered yet another setback when our franchise quarterback, Drew Bledsoe, was knocked out of the game in a loss to the New York Jets. At that time, there wasn't an abundance of optimism for Patriots fans.

Enter Tom Brady.

From the day I bought the team, I was driven to do whatever I could to change the culture of the Patriots and bring a championship to New England. Little did I know the impact a sixth round draft pick in just his second year would have in achieving those goals. The play of Brady and the selfless contributions of so many players on that team underscored the importance of teamwork, as we found ways to beat teams with more talent on a weekly basis, gaining confidence with each of the season-ending nine consecutive victories en route to our first championship.

I believe the adversities we overcame early in the year unified the team. That season, we were the underdog that went on a Cinderella story-like playoff run. No one expected our success. It was earned through everyone's collective contributions. Down the stretch of the regular season and throughout the playoffs, our formula for success was never the same. Offense, defense and special teams each took turns in finding a way to win. We weren't a team loaded with Pro Bowl players and rarely fielded the team with the most individual talent, but we ended up having the most talented team that year.

One of the most memorable moments from that year's Super Bowl was when the Patriots elected to be introduced as a team, in contrast to the traditional introductions of the offensive or defensive starters. It wasn't the reason we won the game, but looking back, it underscored the importance of teamwork and unity prior to the most important game in our franchise's history. I couldn't have scripted a more unbelievable ending to the season. To me, it was remarkably fitting that in the year of 9/11, the team called the Patriots wearing red, white and blue won the Super Bowl. It was especially memorable to do so on an Adam Vinatieri 48-yard field goal as time expired. I know Patriots fans throughout New England were euphoric, but I think that night fans throughout America were proud to celebrate a Patriots victory.

Bringing a championship home to New England to celebrate with more than a million people in the streets of downtown Boston – on the coldest day of the year – was something I will never forget and something I couldn't wait to do again. It provided motivation to push ourselves to new heights. I am sure it motivated the other teams in Boston, too, just as it would have done for us. The taste of success, and the understanding of what a championship can do for a team, a fan base, a city and an entire region makes you want it even more. When you want it more, you do the little things. After you're privileged enough to make it happen once, you become even more driven to make it happen again. As hard as it is to achieve success, it is much harder to sustain it.

I hope that the 2001 Patriots were a catalyst for the many sports championships that followed. In a 15-year span, the Patriots won five of seven Super Bowls. The Red Sox won three World Series titles. The Bruins won a Stanley Cup and the Celtics won an NBA Championship. There's no other city in America that compares. It was great to see each of those championship celebrations unify our communities, bringing people from all backgrounds, all ethnicities, all races and all genders together in celebration.

For much of my life, New England sports fans always hoped for the best but expected the worst. It was a conditioned response after coming close so many times, only to be let down in the end. In Super Bowl XXXVI, while we were leading 17-3 over the highly-favored St. Louis Rams, I remember turning to my family and saying for the first time, "We've got a real shot at doing this!" Soon thereafter, Tebucky Jones picked up a Kurt Warner fumble and ran it back 97 yards for a touchdown. At that moment, just when it looked like we had a three-score lead, the play was called back because of a holding call against Willie McGinest. The Rams scored two plays later to make it a one-possession game at 17-10. I truly feared that was going to be the Patriots' "Bill Buckner moment." The Rams ended up tying the game at 17-all with just 90 second remaining in the game. Fortunately, Brady orchestrated a final drive to put Adam Vinatieri in position to kick a game-winning 48-yard field goal as time expired. It was one of the most dramatic endings in Super Bowl history. Winning that first championship was a moment I will never forget and one shared with millions of other Patriots fans.

The many successes and celebrations by our Boston teams since 2001 have changed the mood and mindset of our fans. Fans no longer fear the worst. In fact, I think they've come to expect the very best. My grandchildren have grown up in an era in Boston where everyone has won. The concept of a "Bill Buckner moment" is foreign to them! And that's a great thing.

At the time, winning Super Bowl XXXVI in 2001 was the greatest moment in the Patriots' 42-year history. I didn't know how it could ever get better than that game-winning kick. But, going 17-2 and winning back-to-back Super Bowls in 2003 and 2004 – each by three-point margins – challenged that notion. I can remember thinking after winning three Super Bowls in four years that it may never get better. Yet, when Malcolm Butler made his game-saving interception at the goal line in Super Bowl XLIX, I couldn't believe that there would ever be a more dramatic ending to a Super Bowl.

Two years later, I was proven wrong. You may have heard me call our fifth Super Bowl title "unequivocally the sweetest," and it was. When we were down 28-3 with less than three minutes to play in the third quarter, we had a 99.6 percent probability of losing that game. It seemed inevitable, but our coaches and players never gave up. Just when it looked like the game was out of reach, Dont'a Hightower delivered with a strip sack of Matt Ryan. Julian Edelman made an incredible catch and Trey Flowers came up with a big sack that pushed Atlanta out of field goal range late in the game. Down by 16, we scored touchdowns on back-to-back drives and converted consecutive two-point conversions to tie the game. It was an amazing display of resiliency and teamwork. Once we tied the game with less than a minute remaining to force the game into overtime, I knew we were going to win. Luckily, Matthew Slater called heads, we won the toss, and once again Brady led the Patriots on a game winning drive in the Super Bowl.

Even after being a part of some of the most memorable games in sports history, I still pinch myself every day to make sure I am not dreaming. It is such a blessing and a privilege to own the Patriots here in my hometown. I was just a little kid from Fuller Street in Brookline. I remember attending games at each of the venues the team played in in Boston. I remember the excitement I had the day I bought season tickets in 1971. I remember sitting in section 212 of the old Schaefer Stadium with my family, dreaming that one day I could own and operate the team that I loved. I remember thinking, "If I ever get the chance …" Well, that chance came on January 21, 1994 when I bought the Patriots for what was, at the time, the highest price ever paid for a sports franchise anywhere in the world. My sweetheart, Myra, thought I was absolutely crazy. But I promised her that if we did a good job of managing the team it would be more impactful than any charitable donations we could make because we could do so much for the emotional well-being of the community. We could bring joy, foster a sense of community to an entire region and inspire people by our dedication, on and off the field, if we did it right. I believed then and I continue to believe to this day that anyone who's privileged enough to own a sports franchise, especially in a region where the fans are so passionate about their teams, assumes the role of custodian of a public asset. We take that role very seriously.

Believe me, I know how lucky I am and how great our fans are. This journey has been pretty special for all of New England. It's also been special to me personally because I'm not just the owner of the New England Patriots; I'm a lifelong fan of New England sports. There is no other city, no other region, no other fanbase of which I'd rather be a part. I go back with the Celtics to Bob Cousy and Bill Sharman. Bill Russell and Jim Loscutoff. I remember Ted Williams getting settled in the batter's box. The year of Yaz! Carlton Fisk motioning that home run ball fair and Bobby Orr flying through the air after his Stanley Cup-clinching goal. Boston has had so many great sports moments in its storied history, and we've had some exceptional ones packed into the past decade and a half. I know there are countless more to come. And we'll all be cheering, as New England, together!

—Robert Kraft, September 2017

➤ INTRODUCTION

I can remember the late 80s and thinking these just might be the good old days for Boston sports fans. In 1986 alone, **the Celtics won their 16th championship**, the Patriots went to the Super Bowl, and the Red Sox went to the World Series. Sure, the Red Sox got "Bucknered" and lost in gut-wrenching fashion, and the Patriots were crushed by "da Bears," 46–10, but at least the Boston teams were getting to the playoffs, and having some success. In 1987, the Celtics lost in the NBA Finals. The following year, they made it to the Eastern

➤ Boston Celtics players Larry Bird, center with sign, Sam Vincent (at left with banner and dark glasses), and Rick Carlisle, right, reaching to fan, ride the parade truck through the streets of Boston, June 10, 1986, during the city's celebration of the team's 16th NBA Championship title. AP PHOTO/PAUL BENOIT

Conference Finals, while the Red Sox went to the American League Championship Series, and the Bruins advanced all the way to the Stanley Cup Finals—before losing. The Bruins returned to the Cup Finals in 1990, and lost again, which meant they had lost five Stanley Cup Finals since their last Cup victory in 1972. So, yes, there was a lot of losing mixed in with the winning, but who should expect more than that?

The more common fan experience is what happened next in Boston sports. The Celtics had seven straight losing seasons in the 90s. The Bruins' run of 29 years making the playoffs ended in 1997 while they went through 11 head coaches in 17 years. After the Red Sox were swept in the 1990 ALCS, they enjoyed only three playoff appearances in 12 years. Along the way, they lost 13 consecutive playoff games, which I have to believe is a record that will never be broken in any sport. And the Patriots endured seven non-playoff seasons in a row from 1987 to 1993. Included in their incompetence were seasons of 1-15 and 2-14. Robert Kraft purchased the team in 1994, and they returned to the playoffs that year, coincidentally losing the wild card game to Bill Belichick's Cleveland Browns.

That was Belichick's only playoff appearance and only playoff victory in five years with the Browns. He beat his former boss, Bill Parcells, in that game, and then eventually teamed up with Parcells as the Patriots assistant head coach in 1996. Together they led the Patriots to the Super Bowl against the

Worthwhile Gambles

"I would say not only what they did for the Patriots and the program and this organization," Belichick said of the 2001 Patriots, "but it was kind of a springboard for Boston sports over that decade. Not that we had anything to do with the Red Sox or the Celtics or the Bruins or anything else, but it was just the first one of many with those three great organizations. You kind of feel proud that we were the first one, and that they all followed."

It turns out the gambles of Kraft and Belichick paid off big time!

> New York Jets defensive coordinator Bill Belichick, center, talks with Jets linebacker Bryan Cox (51) on the sideline as head coach Bill Parcells stands in the background during a game against the Indianapolis Colts at Giants Stadium in East Rutherford, N.J. Oct. 17, 1999. Belichick quit Tuesday, Jan. 4, 2000, as head coach of the New York Jets, one day after being elevated to the job when Parcells resigned. AP PHOTO/JOHN T. GREILICK

Green Bay Packers. **Parcells and Belichick then went to the New York Jets and held the same positions from 1997 to 1999.** Parcells retired and handed the reins to Belichick, who was the head coach of the Jets for all of one day. On January 4, 2000, at the press conference to formally announce his promotion, Belichick instead announced he was resigning. He was hired by the Patriots 23 days later after the Patriots agreed to compensate the Jets with a first-round pick in the upcoming draft, and a fourth- and seventh-rounder in 2002.

"For a number one draft choice," Kraft said, "we can bring in a man that I feel certain can do something, rather than the uncertainty of a draft choice. And it wasn't even close when I thought about it that way."

It was still quite a gamble by the Patriots. Belichick's record as a head coach was just 41-55 in six seasons. He had one playoff appearance with the Cleveland Browns, and only one playoff victory. His track record to this point was, shall we say, unproven. Plus, he had just abruptly resigned from the Jets, and he had a reputation for having poor relationship skills. But Robert Kraft had faith and vision, and he gave Belichick total control of the Patriots' football operations. Belichick's Patriots went 5-11 in his first season, dropped the season opener in 2001, and then they lost their starting quarterback, Drew Bledsoe, to a life-threatening injury while falling to 0-2. It sure didn't look good for the Patriots, or for Robert Kraft's gamble, but Belichick had taken his own gamble. Not only did he draft a quarterback with the 199th pick in 2000, he kept that gangly kid as one of four quarterbacks on the Patriots roster. Just as Kraft saw something in Belichick, Belichick saw something in Tom Brady, and those three men changed the course of history for the New England Patriots and quite possibly for the other three major Boston sports teams.

CHAPTER ONE

THE

THE 2001 NEW ENGLAND PATRIOTS

Owner:
Robert Kraft

Director of Player Personnel:
Scott Pioli

Head Coach:
Bill Belichick

Regular Season Record:
11-5

Regular Season Finish:
AFC East Champions

Playoff Results:
Divisional Round—New England Patriots 16
Oakland Raiders 13 (OT)

AFC Championship—New England Patriots 24
Pittsburgh Steelers 17

Super Bowl:
New England Patriots 20
St. Louis Rams 17

Awards:
Super Bowl MVP: QB Tom Brady

Pro Bowlers: QB Tom Brady, CB Ty Law,
SS Lawyer Milloy, KR Troy Brown

This is not how a dynasty would be expected to begin. Drew Bledsoe, the face of the Patriot franchise and a three-time Pro Bowl quarterback who had signed a 10-year, $103 million contract during the offseason, was laid out on the sideline in the fourth quarter of the second game of the season. The sheared blood vessel he suffered in his chest put Bledsoe in the hospital and Tom Brady behind center. **Brady, the 199th player chosen in the 2000 draft, rose up off the bench like a newborn foal standing for the first time.** Pressed into emergency service, Brady was only able to complete 5 of 10 passes for 46 yards as the Patriots fell to 0-2, losing to the Jets, 10–3. What happened next is the stuff of legends—in particular the legends of Tom Brady and Bill Belichick!

In Week 3 of the 2001 season, Brady made his first NFL start. The tall, lanky 24-year-old who came to New England by way of San Mateo, California, and the University of Michigan, was matched up against Peyton Manning and the Indianapolis Colts. Manning was only one year older than Brady, but already had three full NFL seasons under his belt and was making his 51st career start. He had been the number 1 overall pick in the 1998

> New England Patriots quarterback Tom Brady (12) warms up for play in an NFL game in 2001. AP PHOTO/AL MESSERSCHMIDT

NFL Draft. Manning had the pedigree and the experience, but he would lose 11 of the 17 head-to-head meetings with Brady, including this first one, 44–13. The Patriots rallied around Brady in his first start with the defense forcing four turnovers, running two interceptions back for touchdowns, and sealing the game with three fourth quarter touchdowns. It was the Patriots' first win of the season, and the first win of the Brady era. Brady threw for a very pedestrian 168 yards without a touchdown, but Patriots fans quickly found someone they could believe in. Brady performed as a conservative, mistake-free, game manager and let his defense and running game dominate the Colts. That would have been enough to win over most Patriots fans, but then Brady did even more.

After a loss in Miami, the Patriots came home to face the San Diego Chargers. The Patriots trailed by 10 points with under seven minutes to go, but Brady engineered a field goal drive and then threw a game-tying touchdown to Jermaine Wiggins to force overtime. The Patriots ultimately won the game, 29–26, when Adam Vinatieri kicked a 44-yard field goal. It was another unlikely and unexpected win, and this time, Brady led the way with poise and a touch of magic.

The magic continued with a second trouncing of the Colts, who were playing in the AFC East along with the Patriots for the 31st and final season. The second meeting between the division rivals was in Indianapolis, and this time the magic was provided by wide receiver David Patten, who became the first player since Walter Payton 22 years earlier to run, catch, and throw for a touchdown in the same game. And Patten did it all in the first half!

After the Patriots blocked a Colts field goal attempt and ran the ball back to the Colts' 29-yard line, Patten was handed the ball on the Patriots' first offensive play, and he ran for a touchdown.

Patriot Super Bowl History

Before the 2001 season, the Patriots had been to two Super Bowls, and lost them both. On January 26, 1986, the Patriots lost Super Bowl XX to the Chicago Bears, 46-10, and on January 26, 1997, the Patriots lost Super Bowl XXXI to the Green Bay Packers, 35-21.

In the second quarter, Patten hauled in a 91-yard touchdown pass from Brady, which was the longest play in franchise history. And on the first play of the Patriots' next possession, Patten threw a 60-yard touchdown pass to Troy Brown. With Pro Bowl wide receiver Terry Glenn out with a hamstring injury, Patten's role against the Colts expanded, and he responded in spectacular fashion. With a second touchdown reception, Patten was part of four of the Patriots' five touchdowns.

"Every time I touched the ball, I was able to make something happen," Patten said. "I think I'm able to do that every time I go on the field, and today I made that happen."

The Patriots won 38–17, but were just 3-3 on the season, and they'd dip below .500 the following week when they lost to the Broncos. Playing at Invesco Field at Mile High Stadium in Denver for the first time, Brady had his worst game as a pro. Remarkably, Brady had set a record by beginning his career with 162 consecutive passes without an interception, but he threw four picks in Denver, all of them in the fourth quarter when the Patriots were trying to come from behind. The most costly mistake came with the Patriots trailing, 24–20. Brady led the Patriots to the Denver 8-yard line, but then was picked off in the end zone by the Broncos' Denard Walker. Then, with 2:24 to go, Walker picked off Brady a second time and returned the ball 39 yards for a game-clinching touchdown. The Patriots lost, 31–20, but left Denver with more confidence than they had when they arrived.

"Denver deserved to win," Bill Belichick said after the game, "but I think we know we can beat them."

Even Belichick would have no way of knowing, but the Patriots were approaching the horizon of their miraculous season. Following the loss in Denver, the Patriots were back on the road the following week against the Atlanta Falcons. It was a game that featured nine quarterback sacks by a dominating

Patriot defense, and a bounce-back performance by Brady, who had three touchdown passes. Brady's third touchdown throw came with a bit of luck. In the final minute of the third quarter, he threw deep to Patten, but the ball was tipped away by Falcons defender Ashley Ambrose. However, the tipped ball went right into the arms of Troy Brown, who took it 23 yards to the end zone. The Patriots went on to win, 24–10.

They were just an average 4-4 team, and nothing suggested otherwise when they struggled at home to beat the 1-6 Buffalo Bills the following week. The Bills sacked Brady seven times, intercepted him once, and forced him to fumble twice, and the game wasn't secured until Antowain Smith broke a couple of tackles and ran 42 yards for a touchdown with under two minutes to play. The Patriots escaped with a 21–11 win, putting them over the .500 mark for the first time in three seasons.

Next came the 7-1 St. Louis Rams, which seemed an unlikely Super Bowl preview at the time, if only because the Patriots didn't appear to be Super Bowl bound. The Rams, meanwhile, known as "The Greatest Show on Turf," and boasting the highest-scoring offense in the NFL, came to Foxborough and amassed nearly 500 yards of offense. Still, the Patriots had plenty of chances to pull off the upset.

"We just missed too many opportunities," Belichick said. "Both sides made some plays, but in the end, we just didn't make enough of them. That's real disappointing."

Patriot cornerback Terrell Buckley made an important play in the first quarter when he ran a Kurt Warner pass back 52 yards for a game-tying touchdown. The Patriots seemed poised to take a lead into halftime, but the momentum shifted when Antowain Smith fumbled at the Rams' 3-yard line. Instead of going in for a touchdown, or at the very least kicking a field goal with time winding down in the half, the Patriots committed one of their three costly turnovers. The Rams took possession with 2:22 to go in the half and drove the ball 97 yards. Warner connected with Marshall Faulk for a 9-yard touchdown pass, and instead of trailing at the break, the Rams were ahead 14–10. The Patriots would ultimately fall, 24–17, and rested at an unspectacular 5-5.

In the days leading up to the Rams game, the Patriots learned that Bledsoe had been medically cleared to play, but after having Bledsoe and Brady split snaps in practice, Belichick chose to start Brady against the Rams. Then, after Brady threw for 185 yards with one touchdown and two interceptions against the Rams, Belichick announced his decision to keep Brady as the starter for the rest of the season "barring unforeseen circumstances."

"It is game to game, but I don't see how it's going to change," Belichick said. "It's not going to be, 'There's an incomplete pass. We're going to change quarterbacks.' We can't operate like that."

On Being a Team

❝It's not about who plays or who doesn't play," Bledsoe would say later. "It's about who wins, and I'll do what I can to help this team win.**❞**

The Patriots, who had gone 5-11 the previous year with Bledsoe as the starter, and then got off to an 0-2 start, were 5-3 with Brady as their starting quarterback. Belichick reasoned that Brady gave the Patriots their best chance moving forward, and by making the announcement he avoided the potential of a weekly quarterback controversy.

With Bledsoe accepting the disappointment as a consummate professional, the Patriots entered the final six weeks of the season unified, and Brady made sure that Belichick's huge gamble was the right call. In the first game after the decision, Brady threw a career-high four touchdown passes against the New Orleans Saints. The Patriots beat the Saints, 38–17, and won the five regular-season games that followed. They would roll into the playoffs with the momentum of a six-game winning streak, but Brady never looked as good again as he did against the Saints. In fact, in the Patriots' last five games, Brady threw five interceptions and only two touchdown passes. But the Patriots kept winning!

They rallied from 13 points down in the first half to beat the Jets, 17–16, and good fortune was still driving the bus when

› New England Patriots kicker Adam Vinatieri is all smiles as he celebrates his overtime field goal with coach Bill Belichick after the game at Ralph Wilson Stadium in Orchard Park, N.Y., Sunday, Dec. 16, 2001. The Patriots won 12–9. AP PHOTO/MIKE GROLL

the Patriots beat the Bills in overtime in Week 14. Late in that game, David Patten caught a pass along the sideline and was immediately hit hard enough to cause him to fumble and to lose consciousness. The Bills recovered the ball, but upon review, it was ruled that while Patten lay there, the ball touched his feet while his head was out of bounds. By rule, the ball was dead. **The Bills did not gain possession! Instead, the Patriots went on to kick a 23-yard field goal to win the game, 12–9.**

The winning streak continued with wins against the Dolphins, 20–13, and the Carolina Panthers, 38–6. And as it turned out, the unconscious player touching the ball while his head was out of bounds wouldn't be the strangest call to go in the Patriots' favor. The long, strange trip that would be the Patriots' journey to the franchise's first Super Bowl victory would continue the following weekend on a snowy night in Foxborough.

The divisional round playoff game against the Oakland Raiders would be the final game ever played at Foxboro Stadium, and it would include one of the most controversial calls in the history of the NFL playoffs. Longtime, diehard football fans who had watched thousands of hours of football were introduced to the "tuck rule." At a pivotal moment late in the fourth quarter with the Patriots trailing, 13–10, Brady appeared to fumble the ball, which was recovered by the Raiders. However, instant replay showed that Brady had started his arm forward as if to pass, and then changed his mind **and attempted to tuck the ball under his arm.** By rule, now known as the "tuck rule," Brady did not fumble. Instead, it was ruled an

> Patriots quarterback Tom Brady (12) loses the ball after being brought down by Oakland Raiders' Charles Woodson, right, while Greg Biekert (54) moves to recover the ball in the fourth quarter of their AFC Division Playoff game in Foxborough, Mass. Saturday night, Jan. 19, 2002. The play was appealed, and the Patriots retained possession. The Patriots went on to win 16–13, in overtime. AP PHOTO/ELISE AMENDOLA

incomplete pass, and the Patriots maintained possession of the ball. The drive continued and Adam Vinatieri eventually tied the game with a 45-yard field goal in a driving snowstorm. It is considered by many to be the greatest kick in NFL history.

The Patriots won the coin toss to start overtime and chose to receive the ball. Despite the wind blowing and the snow falling, the Patriots came out throwing. Brady completed seven consecutive passes, but faced a fourth-and-4 from the Raiders' 34-yard line. He made it eight straight completions by connecting with David Patten for six yards and a first down. The Patriots then ran five straight running plays and moved the ball to the Raiders' 7-yard line. On third down, the Patriots sent out the field goal unit. The Raiders called timeout, which gave Patriots holder Ken Walter and Vinatieri time to clear away the snow from the spot where the ball would be placed, and then **Vinatieri kicked a 23-yard game-winning field goal that was punctuated by long snapper Lonie Paxton's snow angel in the end**

Player Shifts

Following the 2001 season, Drew Bledsoe was traded to the Buffalo Bills for their 2003 first-round draft pick. That pick was subsequently traded along with a sixth-round pick to the Chicago Bears for defensive tackle Ty Warren.

> New England Patriots kicker Adam Vinatieri, top, is hoisted to the shoulders of his teammates after his game-winning overtime field goal against the Oakland Raiders in the AFC Divisional Playoff game at Foxboro Stadium, in Foxborough, Mass., Saturday Jan. 19, 2002. The Patriots won 16–13.
AP PHOTO/CHARLES KRUPA

zone. While his teammates danced around him, Paxton flapped away, his arms looking like thick windshield wipers. The following week, the Patriots season would continue with yet another improbable story line: Drew Bledsoe returned to help defeat the Steelers in Pittsburgh.

The season that began with Bledsoe getting hurt and Brady taking over the quarterback reins wouldn't end until Bledsoe was back up on the horse. The turnabout occurred in the AFC championship game at Heinz Field in Pittsburgh. Brady was knocked out of the game with a sprained ankle late in the second quarter**, and that opened the door for Bledsoe's return. Three quick completions to David Patten, the last one in the end zone,** and the Patriots had a 14–3 halftime lead.

In the third quarter, the Patriots' Brandon Mitchell blocked a field goal attempt and Troy Brown scooped up the loose ball. Brown, who had a 55-yard punt return for a touchdown in the first quarter, ran a few yards with the ball before lateraling it to Antwan Harris, and Harris took it the remaining 49 yards for the touchdown. With the help of their Pro Bowl backup quar-

> New England Patriots quarterback Drew Bledsoe signals from the line during their AFC Championship game against the Pittsburgh Steelers Sunday, Jan. 27, 2002, in Pittsburgh. AP PHOTO/AMY SANCETTA

> New England Patriots wide receiver David Patten (86) pulls in an 11-yard touchdown pass from quarterback Drew Bledsoe as Pittsburgh Steelers Jason Gildon (92) defends in the second quarter of the AFC Championship game Sunday, Jan. 27, 2002, in Pittsburgh. Bledsoe, playing for the first time in more than four months, lofted the ball to Patten deep in the right corner of the end zone. AP PHOTO/CHRIS GARDNER

terback and two special teams touchdowns, the Patriots held on to win, 24–17. The Patriots were headed to the Super Bowl with the same cloud of a quarterback controversy hovering over the team that was there when Bledsoe was first cleared to play, and once again Belichick chose Brady over Bledsoe.

Without the built-in advantage of two weeks between the AFC championship game and the Super Bowl that teams often have, Belichick had just a few days to make his decision. With Brady's ankle heavily taped, Belichick put the quarterbacks through a rigorous practice on the Tuesday before the game. Brady's ankle held up well and Belichick made the decision to have Brady start the Super Bowl against the St. Louis Rams. Bledsoe took the news in stride.

"I'm obviously very disappointed," Bledsoe told reporters. "It's something I probably expected, to be honest with you. But I'll do everything I can to help Tom win the game."

➤ New England Patriots cornerback Ty Law (24) intercepts a pass from St. Louis Rams quarterback Kurt Warner as intended receiver Isaac Bruce (80) looks on during Super Bowl XXXVI, Sunday, Feb. 3, 2002, in New Orleans. Law returned the interception for a touchdown.
AP PHOTO/TONY GUTIERREZ

But the greatest help Brady got in Super Bowl XXXVI came from his defense. Facing the 14-2 Rams for a second time, this time at the Louisiana Superdome in New Orleans, the Patriots once again forced three turnovers and scored on an interception return. **Ty Law grabbed a Kurt Warner pass and took it back untouched 47 yards for the touchdown to give the Patriots a 7–3 lead in the second quarter.** Later, Terrell Buckley recovered a Ricky Proehl fumble and the Patriots converted that into an 8-yard touchdown pass from Tom Brady to David Patten with 21 seconds remaining in the first half. The Patriots led 14–3, and after Otis Smith intercepted Warner in the third quarter, and returned the ball to the Rams' 33, Vinatieri would boot a field goal to give the Patriots a two-touchdown lead. The Rams responded with a short rushing touchdown by Warner, and a 26-yard touchdown pass from Warner to Proehl, and the game was tied 17–17 with 1:30 to go.

Instead of running out the clock and taking the game to overtime, the Patriots put the ball in the hands of their first-year starter, ran their two-minute offense, and tried to win the game. **Brady completed 7 of 9 passes** (both incompletions were spikes to stop the clock),

> New England Patriots Tom Brady plays in Super Bowl XXXVI against the St. Louis Rams at the Louisiana Superdome on February 3, 2002, in New Orleans. The Patriots defeated the Rams 20–17. AP PHOTO/TOM DIPACE

Duck Boat Parade

"Cue the duck boats!" would quickly become a rallying cry for New England. Duck Boat Tours, a privately owned company with a fleet of amphibious vehicles, began a tradition of transporting a newly crowned New England championship team over Boston's roads and waterways.

> New England Patriots kicker Adam Vinatieri (4), joined by teammate Ken Walter, who held the ball, celebrates his 48-yard game-winning field goal in the final seconds of Super Bowl XXXVI against the St. Louis Rams, Feb. 3, 2002, in New Orleans. With the score tied at 17–17, and no timeouts remaining, Patriots quarterback Tom Brady had led a last-minute drive downfield to set up Vinatieri's deciding kick. The Patriots won their first Super Bowl 20–17. AP PHOTO/AMY SANCETTA

and put the Patriots in field goal range. Once again, Vinatieri jogged on the field and put a clutch kick between the uprights. His 48-yard field goal was **the first time the Super Bowl was ever decided on the game's final play.**

> New England Patriots quarterback Tom Brady, right, wearing red scarf, dances with head coach Bill Belichick, center, in plaid scarf, during a Super Bowl celebration on City Hall Plaza in Boston, Tuesday, Feb. 5, 2002. At far left on stage is Patriots owner Robert Kraft. AP PHOTO/CHARLES KRUPA

> Members of the New England Patriots ride in duck boats down Tremont Street in Boston, Tuesday, Feb. 5, 2002, during a parade held to celebrate the team's Super Bowl win. Hundreds of thousands of New England Patriots fans braved freezing temperatures Tuesday to welcome home the improbable Super Bowl victors and celebrate the city's first championship in 16 years. AP PHOTO/OLIVIA HANLEY

The 2001 New England Patriots were celebrated by land and by sea by more than 1.2 million fans who lined the streets of Boston for what was **the first in a long series of duck boat parades.** The parade route started at Copley Square and settled at City Hall Plaza, where cornerback Ty Law convinced Belichick, Kraft, and Brady to dance on stage. They were all equally bad!

"It's been a long voyage and a long journey," Belichick told the crowd. "We took the last step of the way Sunday night. And I feel like our journey is complete now."

Yes, the journey that was the 2001 NFL season was complete, but the odyssey of the NFL's most unexpected dynasty had just begun.

> New England Patriots fans cheer during a Super Bowl celebration on City Hall Plaza in Boston, Tuesday Feb. 5, 2002. AP PHOTO/JON MAHONEY

CHAPTER TWO

THE
2003 NEW ENGLAND
PATRIOTS

Owner:
Robert Kraft

Vice President of Player Personnel:
Scott Pioli

Head Coach:
Bill Belichick

Regular Season Record:
14-2

Regular Season Finish:
AFC East Champions

Playoff Results:
Divisional Round—New England Patriots 17
Tennessee Titans 14

AFC Championship—New England Patriots 24
Indianapolis Colts 14

Super Bowl:
New England Patriots 32
Carolina Panthers 29

Awards:
Super Bowl MVP: QB Tom Brady

Pro Bowlers: CB Ty Law, LB Willie McGinest,
DE Richard Seymour

The Patriots brought the Lombardi Trophy to Foxborough and opened the 2002 season in a brand-new Gillette Stadium. The Super Bowl banner was raised in front of more than 68,000 fans. Former president George H. W. Bush conducted the pregame coin toss, and the Patriots beat the Steelers 30–14. It was a euphoric grand opening of a new stadium, and a new year began with renewed hope. Brady and the Patriots won the first three games while scoring 115 points, but when the offense sputtered, they lost the next four games. Ultimately, they finished in a three-way tie with the Dolphins and Jets, all with 9-7 records. The tiebreaker rules gave the division title to the Jets. This is not the way you'd expect a dynasty to be continued. The Patriots set out to defend their NFL championship, but failed to make the playoffs.

It was on to 2003!

Before the Patriot Dynasty finally got rolling, there was one more giant speed bump to go over. The Patriots began the 2003 season by losing to the Buffalo Bills, 31–0. The game was played in Orchard Park, New York, five days after the Patriots released popular Pro Bowl safety Lawyer Milloy. It was a stunning move given Milloy's talent and the respect he commanded from his teammates. He wasn't out of work for long, however. The Bills scooped him up and put him in the starting lineup in Week 1 against his old team. Milloy's impact was felt immediately. He sacked Brady once, and forced him to throw one of his four interceptions. Brady summed up the game this way: "From the first play on, it was Buffalo, Buffalo, Buffalo."

But the rest of the 2003 season was Patriots, Patriots, Patriots! They won 14 of the next 15 games, including three by shutout. One of those shutouts came on the final weekend of the season, and it remains one of the most bizarre statistical anomalies in the history of sports. The Patriots, who lost to the Bills 31–0 to start the season, closed the season by beating the Bills by the exact same score. **Brady, who threw four interceptions in that season opener, threw four touchdown passes in the season finale.**

> New England Patriots quarterback and game MVP Tom Brady (12) celebrates a touchdown during Super Bowl XXXVIII against the Carolina Panthers, Feb. 1, 2004 in Houston.
AP PHOTO/GREG TROTT

Bouncing back quickly from the loss to the Bills, the Patriots showcased in Week 2 against the Philadelphia Eagles what would become a dominating defense. The Patriots forced six turnovers, had seven sacks, and rolled to a 31–10 victory. Patriot tight end Christian Fauria caught two touchdown passes in the second quarter, and Brady threw his third touchdown pass, a 26-yarder to Deion Branch, in the third quarter. Tedy Bruschi closed out the scoring with an 18-yard interception return.

"We played better. We executed better. We scored in the red area and we played better defense in the red area," Bill Belichick said. "It's not that complicated."

The defense was stout once again the following week in a 23–16 home opening win against the Jets. The Patriots ultimately sealed the deal with a 55-yard interception return for a touchdown by rookie cornerback Asante Samuel.

A Week 4 loss to the Washington Redskins dropped the Patriots to 2-2. Brady threw three more interceptions and a Kevin Faulk fumble accounted for the Patriots' fourth turnover. The Patriots, playing without nine starters from their season-opening lineup, battled back from 20–3 down, but decided to forgo a possible 55-yard game-tying field goal in the closing seconds. Instead, Brady threw an incomplete pass on fourth down, and the Patriots lost 20–17. It was one of only five wins the Redskins would secure that year. The Patriots did not appear

> New England Patriots defensive back Ty Law (24) during preseason game against the Philadelphia Eagles at Lincoln Financial Field in Philadelphia, Pennsylvania on August 8, 2003. The Patriots defeated the Eagles 24–12. TOMASSO DEROSA VIA AP

to be a juggernaut in waiting. But following the loss to the Redskins, the Patriots embarked upon a 21-game winning streak. It began with a hard-fought 38–30 win over the Titans in Week 5. Patriot safety Rodney Harrison characterized it as "one of the more intense games" he had ever played. **Injured cornerback Ty Law, running on a severely sprained right ankle, iced the victory** with a 65-yard interception return for a touchdown with just under two minutes to play. The following week, the Patriots improved to 4-2 when four more interceptions helped them get past the New York Giants, 17–6. **The Giants turned the ball over a total of five times,** including twice on their first three offensive plays. The second one was a 38-yard fumble return for a touchdown by Patriots linebacker Matt Chatham. Brady completed only one pass for 7 yards during a first half played in heavy rains and finished with just 112 yards passing, but the Patriots didn't have any turnovers.

> New England Patriots linebacker Matt Chatham (58) races to the end zone with a picked-up fumble during the first quarter at Gillette Stadium as teammates Willie McGinest (55), Richard Seymour (93) and Bobby Hamilton (91) run behind him Sunday, Oct. 12, 2003, in Foxborough, Mass. Chatham returned the fumble for a touchdown. AP PHOTO/STEPHAN SAVOIA

The Patriots extended their winning streak to three games and took over first place in the AFC East when they survived the "Lady Columbia" overtime thriller in Miami in Week 7. The Patriots and Dolphins went to overtime and the coin toss became a point of controversy. The Patriots called tails and when the coin flip on the silver dollar showed Lady Columbia, the Patriots thought they'd won. But Lady Columbia was designated as tails. The Dolphins chose to receive the ball, which meant the Patriots would choose the direction they wanted to kick off. And in case of a game-winning field goal attempt, the Patriots wanted the Dolphins to be kicking on the same side of the field where Dolphins placekicker Olindo Mare had a 35-yard field goal attempt blocked by Richard Seymour with less than two minutes to go in regulation. That side of the field was covered by dirt, because the Florida Marlins were hosting the Major League Baseball playoffs at the same stadium. The Dolphins did move the ball into Patriots territory, and once again set up for a 35-yard field goal attempt from the dirt. Mare, the second most accurate field goal kicker in NFL history, missed again! The Patriots got the ball, but had to punt it back to the Dolphins, who gave it right back to the Patriots. Miami quarterback Jay Fiedler lobbed a 60-yard duck that came down in the arms of Patriot cornerback Tyrone Poole. The Patriots had another chance! And it didn't take long for them to take advantage of it. **Brady threw an 82-yard touchdown pass to Troy Brown.** The Patriots flew home from Miami with a 19–13 win.

› New England Patriots wide receiver Troy Brown, right, outruns Miami Dolphins safeties Sammy Knight, left, and Brock Marion for a touchdown in overtime to beat the Dolphins 19–13 Sunday, Oct. 19, 2003, in Miami. AP PHOTO/J. PAT CARTER

It was the first time in 13 years they were able to beat the Dolphins in Miami during September or October.

"Everyone's telling them they can't win down here, everyone's telling them it's too hot. Everyone's telling them they have too many injuries," Belichick said. "They didn't buy it. They came down and played their hearts out. It felt good."

The following week, the Patriots were held out of the end zone, but still managed to beat the Browns, 9–3. That set up a Monday night showdown with the Broncos in Denver, where the Patriots had only one win in their last 13 trips. And if **the legend of Bill Belichick** wasn't already approaching mythical proportions, this game would put him front and center in the "best coaches ever" conversation. Already with a Super Bowl ring as a head coach and two others as a defensive coordinator with the Giants, Belichick engineered an exciting and unlikely comeback against the Broncos. Trailing 24–23 in the fourth quarter, and backed up on their own

> New England Patriots coach Bill Belichick reacts on the sidelines in the first quarter against the Dallas Cowboys in Foxborough, Mass., Sunday, Nov. 16, 2003. AP PHOTO/ELISE AMENDOLA

> New England Patriots wide receiver David Givens (87) catches an 18-yard touchdown against Denver Broncos safety Deltha O'Neal (24) in the closing minute of the game to give the Patriots a 30–26 win in Denver, Monday, Nov. 3, 2003. AP PHOTO/DAVID ZALUBOWSKI

1-yard line, the Patriots were forced to punt—only they didn't! Instead of punting, Belichick instructed long snapper Lonie Paxton to snap the ball out of the end zone. That would give the Broncos two points for the safety and a three-point lead, but the Patriots would be able to punt the ball from their 20-yard line instead of the back of their end zone.

"We were hoping to get the ball back in decent field position and still have some time to at least try for a field goal to tie it," Belichick explained.

And it worked! The Patriots forced a three-and-out from the Broncos, and then got the ball back at their own 42-yard line with 2:15 left in the game. Because of the intentional safety, the Patriots would only need to go about 25 yards to try for a game-tying field goal. The strategy had paid off, but the kick was never necessary. Instead, with 30 seconds remaining, Brady won the game with an **18-yard touchdown pass to David Givens**. The Patriots' gamble paid off and they beat the Broncos 30–26. The intentional safety has got to be one of the greatest in-game decisions by a coach ever!

The Patriots were back home in Week 11, and they put their five-game winning streak to the test against former head coach Bill Parcells and his 7-2 Dallas Cowboys. It was another defensive struggle won by the Patriots, who intercepted Dallas quarterback Quincy Carter three times, two of them by Ty Law. The Patriot offense struggled, but their defense pitched a shutout and the winning streak extended to six games with a 12–0 win.

The following week in Houston, Brady threw two interceptions and lost a fumble, the Patriots had a punt blocked, and missed a field goal, but still managed to win their seventh game in a row. The biggest call of the game came with 40 seconds to play and the Patriots down 20–13. On fourth-and-1 from the 4-yard line, the Patriots decided to throw the ball and go for the game-tying touchdown. Brady rolled to his right and threw **a 4-yard touchdown →** **pass to tight end Daniel Graham**. In overtime, the Texans won the coin toss and elected to receive the ball, but on their first play from scrimmage, Patriot linebacker Mike Vrabel intercepted a pass by Houston quarterback Tony Banks. That gave the Patriots the ball at Houston's 23-yard line. The Patriots set up for the game-winning field goal, opting to run the ball three times in a row. They only got as far as the 19-yard line before bringing Vinatieri in to attempt the game-winning field goal. Vinatieri's

> Daniel Graham of the New England Patriots during the Pats' 21–14 loss to the San Diego Chargers at Qualcomm Stadium in San Diego, Calif. JOHN CORDES/ICON SPORTSWIRE ICON SPORTSWIRE VIA AP IMAGES

kick was blocked! The Patriots relied once again on their defense to give them another chance to win the game, and eventually, with 41 seconds left in overtime, Vinatieri ran back out on to the field and this time, he kicked a 28-yard field goal. The Patriots continued to find ways to win.

In Week 13, the 9-2 Patriots traveled to Indianapolis to face the 9-2 Colts. It would be the third matchup in the Brady-Manning rivalry, and the quarterbacks would lead their teams to a

The One That Got Away-really didn't get away.

❝It didn't look good," Brady conceded later. "When it was first-and-goal at the 2, I was like, 'I can't believe we let this one get away.'**❞**

combined 72 points, but the unsung heroes would be Bethel Johnson and Willie McGinest of the Patriots. Following a Colts touchdown and with just 12 seconds to play in the first half, Johnson stunned the Colts with a 92-yard kickoff return for a touchdown. That gave the Patriots a 24–10 lead, and they would extend the lead to 21 points in the third quarter, but the Colts would erase the deficit on three Manning touchdown passes. A 6-yarder to Troy Walters tied the game at 31–31 with 10:21 to play. After the Walters touchdown, the Patriots struck back quickly when Johnson returned the ensuing kickoff 67 yards. Four plays later, **Brady connected with Troy Brown for a 13-yard touchdown pass.**

> New England Patriots wide receiver Troy Brown (80) catches a pass during a Week 1 NFL football game against the Buffalo Bills at Ralph Wilson Stadium in Orchard Park, New York on September 7, 2003. The Bills defeated the Patriots 31–0.
AP PHOTO/SCOTT BOEHM

With 3:31 to play, the Colts were stopped at the Patriots' 11-yard line and Mike Vanderjagt kicked a field goal to make it 38–34 Patriots. Three Brady incompletions and a shanked punt by Ken Walter gave the Colts the ball back at midfield with three minutes to play. Eventually, the Colts had first-and-goal from the Patriots 2-yard line with 40 seconds to go in the game. A touchdown would win it for the Colts!

But Colts running back Edgerrin James was stuffed twice and Manning threw an incomplete pass, making it fourth-and-1 from the 1, and the goal line stand was complete when McGinest met James in the backfield and tackled him to secure the 38–34 win.

"When you come watch us, you'll see some weird things," Patriot linebacker Tedy Bruschi said.

True enough! The following week, when more than two feet of snow had covered New England, the Patriots and Dolphins struggled to score points at Gillette Stadium. **Bruschi scored the game's only touchdown** when he intercepted a pass and ran it back 5 yards sliding into the end zone on his knees. Fans celebrated by tossing snow into the air, and the Patriots celebrated the AFC East title with a 12–0 win, their ninth victory in a row.

The Patriots sprinted to the finish line of the regular season, collecting seven interceptions against the Jaguars, Jets, and Bills. In the end, the Patriots counted three shutouts among their NFL-best 14 wins, and had two more games in which the opponent failed to score a touchdown. They had the best defense in the NFL, and as they had done two years earlier, the Patriots had gotten hot at the right time.

> New England Patriots' Tedy Bruschi (54) and Matt Chatham (58) celebrate Bruschi's interception for a touchdown against the Miami Dolphins in the fourth quarter in Foxborough, Mass., Sunday, Dec. 7, 2003. Bruschi has been so proficient at getting into the end zone that New England Patriots coach Bill Belichick joked earlier in the season that he might switch the linebacker over to the offense. AP PHOTO/WINSLOW TOWNSON

> New England Patriots' Bethel Johnson runs back a kickoff 92-yards for a touchdown in the final seconds of the second quarter against the Indianapolis Colts in Indianapolis, Sunday, Nov. 30, 2003.
AP PHOTO/DARRON CUMMINGS

In 2001, they went into the playoffs with a six-game winning streak. In 2003, their consecutive-game win streak was at 12 when they welcomed the Titans into Gillette Stadium for the divisional round of the playoffs. With a gametime temperature of 4 degrees and a wind chill of minus 11, it was the coldest game in Patriot franchise history. Four minutes into the game, **Brady connected with Bethel Johnson** on a 41-yard touchdown pass, and with four minutes to go in the game, Vinatieri kicked a 46-yard field goal. In between, running back Antowain Smith had a 1-yard touchdown carry, and the Patriots held on for a 17–14 win.

The Patriots were back in the AFC championship game, and this time they'd face Peyton Manning and the high-powered Colts. Manning had thrown eight touchdown passes the previous two weeks in playoff wins over the Broncos and Chiefs, and the Colts were never forced to punt in either of those two games. The Patriot defense took that as a challenge. With intermittent snow and rain falling, the Patriots forced five Colt turnovers. Manning threw interceptions on the Colts' first two possessions of the game, and when the Colts were finally forced to punt for the first time in the playoffs, the snap went over the punter's head and resulted in a safety. In the end, Manning threw four interceptions, **three of them to Ty Law**. Adam Vinatieri kicked five field goals, and Brady threw a 7-yard touchdown pass to David Givens. The Patriots went on to win, 24–14, and headed to Houston for Super Bowl XXXVIII against the Carolina Panthers.

> Indianapolis Colts quarterback Peyton Manning reacts to the referees not calling holding on one of his receivers during their final drive in the Colts' 24–14 loss to the New England Patriots in the AFC Championship at Gillette Stadium in Foxborough, Mass. Sunday, Jan. 18, 2004.
AP PHOTO/WINSLOW TOWNSON

> New England Patriots Deion Branch (83) reacts after scoring the Patriots' first touchdown on a pass from quarterback Tom Brady against the Carolina Panthers in the second quarter of Super Bowl XXXVIII in Houston, Sunday Feb. 1, 2004. Behind Branch is Panthers' Mike Minter.
AP PHOTO/MORRY GASH

In the Super Bowl that will forever be remembered for Janet Jackson's "wardrobe malfunction" during the halftime show, both offenses started slowly and finished feverishly. There was no score nearly 27 minutes into the game before both teams offered a glimpse of the kind of quick-strike capability that was to come later. With 3:05 to go in the first half, **Brady threw a 5-yard touchdown pass to Deion Branch**. The Panthers responded two minutes later with a 39-yard touchdown from Jake Delhomme to Steve Smith. That left just over a minute to go in the half, which turned out to be enough time for Brady to march the Patriots down the field and hook up with Givens for another 5-yard touchdown. Carolina took over with 18 seconds remaining and moved the ball deep enough into Patriot territory so that John Kasay could kick a 50-yard field goal. Three touchdowns and a field goal in the final three minutes of the half sent the Patriots to the locker room with a 14–10 lead.

All that offensive momentum stalled when the third quarter was as scoreless as the first, but then the teams exploded for five fourth quarter touchdowns. Antowain Smith gave the Patriots a 21–10 lead with a 2-yard touchdown run on the second play of the fourth quarter. Carolina answered with a DeShaun Foster 33-yard touchdown run, but the Panthers failed on a two-point conversion attempt and trailed 21–16. On the Patriots' next possession, Brady was picked off in the end zone by Reggie Howard, and two plays later, Delhomme connected with Muhsin

> New England Patriots kicker Adam Vinatieri celebrates his game-winning field goal with teammate Ken Walter, rear, during the final seconds of their 32–29 victory over the Carolina Panthers in Super Bowl XXXVIII on Sunday, Feb. 1, 2004, at Reliant Stadium in Houston.
AP PHOTO/DAVE MARTIN

Muhammad for an 85-yard touchdown pass, which was the longest play from scrimmage in Super Bowl history. The Panthers had their first lead of the game at 22–21, but for a second time, the Panthers attempted the two-point conversion and failed. The decision to go for two points twice would come back to haunt the Panthers and their head coach, John Fox.

With 2:51 to go, Brady threw a 1-yard touchdown pass to Mike Vrabel, and Kevin Faulk ran in the two-point conversion. The Patriots led 29–22 with under three minutes to play. The Panthers needed only 90 seconds to go 80 yards and score a game-tying touchdown: Delhomme to Ricky Proehl from 12 yards out. That gave the Patriots 1:13 to try for the win. They had all three of their timeouts left, and when Kasay sent the kickoff out of bounds, the Patriots got the ball at their 40-yard line. Five plays and 37 yards later, Brady left it to Vinatieri once again. **Vinatieri, who had missed two attempts earlier in the game, delivered with a 41-yard field goal.** It was the Patriots' 15th straight win and their second Super Bowl title in three years.

"Nobody makes all of them," Belichick said, "But if you've got to have one kick with everything on the line, he's the one you want kicking it. It was an awesome kick. It was a great kick. That's the game. That's what Adam's here for."

Brady was once again voted the Super Bowl MVP. He threw for 354 yards and three touchdowns, and his 32 completions were a Super Bowl record. Another duck boat parade was held, but Patriots safety Rodney Harrison did not attend. He broke his right arm making a tackle on the Panthers' final possession, and when he couldn't get off the field for the next play, he made another tackle with the broken arm. So, instead of rolling through the streets of Boston and hearing the cheers of Patriots fans, Harrison underwent surgery to have a metal plate inserted into his arm. He was the team leader in tackles during the regular season, and Richard Seymour called him "the heart and soul of the team." Harrison made a full recovery and returned to help the Patriots win their third Super Bowl in four years.

> New England Patriots quarterback Tom Brady looks downfield for a receiver during the AFC divisional playoff game against the Tennessee Titans, Saturday, Jan. 10, 2004, in Foxborough, Mass.
AP PHOTO/JIM ROGASH

CHAPTER THREE

THE
2004 BOSTON RED SOX

Principal Owner:
John Henry

General Manager:
Theo Epstein

Manager:
Terry Francona

Regular Season Record:
98-64

Regular Season Finish:
Second in AL East

Playoff Results:
Wild Card Round—Boston Red Sox defeated
Anaheim Angels (3–0)

AL Championship Series—Boston Red Sox
defeated New York Yankees (4–3)

World Series:
Boston Red Sox defeated
St. Louis Cardinals (4–0)

Awards:
World Series MVP: LF Manny Ramirez

All-Stars: OF Manny Ramirez, 1B David Ortiz,
P Curt Schilling

The story of the 2004 Boston Red Sox begins at the end of the 2003 season. The Red Sox and New York Yankees battled for seven games in the American League Championship Series. Game 7 was at Yankee Stadium, and future Hall of Famer Pedro Martínez got the start for the Red Sox. After seven innings, the Red Sox led 5–2, and it was expected that Sox manager Grady Little would take Martínez out of the game. Little chose, instead, to send Martínez back out for the eighth inning. Martínez got the first batter out, but then proceeded to give up four consecutive hits, allowing three runs to score. By the time Little came out to relieve Martínez, the game was tied, 5–5, and it stayed that way until the 11th inning. That's when the Yankees' Aaron Boone stepped up to face knuckleballer Tim Wakefield and hit the first pitch he saw into the seats in left field for a walkoff home run! The Red Sox lost the game, 6–5, and the series 4 games to 3. Grady Little was fired less than two weeks later.

The Red Sox came back in 2004 with a new manager, Terry Francona; a new ace, Curt Schilling; and a new closer, Keith Foulke. Those were the pieces needed to get the Red Sox past the Yankees,

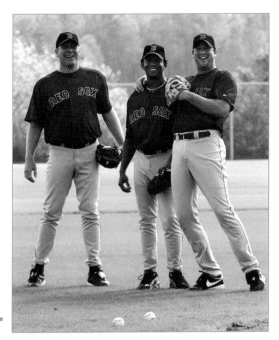

> Boston Red Sox pitchers Curt Schilling, left, Pedro Martinez, and Derek Lowe, right, enjoy a laugh during a pitchers' fielding drill at spring training workouts on Tuesday, Feb. 24, 2004, in Fort Myers, Fla. Schilling, who was acquired from Arizona in a trade, was slated to be the number two starter for Boston, sandwiched between Martinez and Lowe. AP PHOTO/BRITA MENG OUTZEN

> New Boston Red Sox manager Terry Francona smiles as he gives reporters an assesments of workouts for pitchers and catchers at spring training Monday, Feb. 23, 2004, in Fort Myers, Fla. AP PHOTO/JIM MONE

and lift them to their first World Series title in 86 years. The 37-year-old Schilling was acquired in a trade with the Arizona Diamondbacks after Red Sox general manager Theo Epstein spent Thanksgiving at Schilling's home in Arizona and convinced him to waive his no-trade clause. Epstein actually left Thanksgiving dinner without an agreement with Schilling, but a few phone calls over the next 24 hours did the trick. And the Red Sox desperately wanted Schilling. He had won over 20 games twice for the Diamondbacks going a combined 45-13 in 2001 and 2002, and finishing both years second in the Cy Young voting to teammate Randy Johnson. Schilling and Johnson were co-MVPs of the 2001 World Series when the Diamondbacks beat the Yankees, and Epstein and the Red Sox brass were hoping Schilling could team up with another future Hall of Famer, Pedro Martínez, and get them past the Yankees as well. Schilling wanted that, too.

"I want to be a part of bringing the first World Series in modern history to Boston," Schilling said. "And hopefully more than one over the next four years."

Another reason Schilling decided to come to Boston was the likelihood that he would be reunited with Francona, who had managed Schilling when both were with the Phillies from

1997 to 2000. Francona was rumored to be on the short list of managers to replace Little, and indeed, the Red Sox hired him on December 4, 2003, one week after acquiring Schilling. A month later, the Red Sox completed a franchise-altering offseason by signing Foulke, who had been an All-Star in 2003, saving 43 games and going 9-1 for the Oakland A's while Francona was a bench coach. Foulke was a free agent and the Red Sox swooped in and gave him a guaranteed $24 million over three years.

"Just the excitement of playing for a team with this heritage and this history is something I want to do before I retire," Foulke said. "I would love to be part of a championship. Bobby Orr called me and left a message. He said, 'You win in this town, you're forever idolized.' He called me after I met with the Red Sox. I was too scared to call him back."

Epstein recognized the lack of a proven closer had cost the Red Sox dearly in 2003, and that Foulke would fill that void.

World Series Record

The Red Sox won 5 World Series titles from 1903 to 1918. They then lost four straight Game 7's in their World Series appearances in 1946, 1967, 1975, and 1986.

> Keith Foulke, a free agent signed by the Boston Red Sox, throws as spring training workouts began Saturday, Feb. 21, 2004, in Fort Myers, Fla. Foulke, who was 9–1 last season with Oakand, was being considered as the Red Sox closer. AP PHOTO/JIM MONE

"We couldn't be happier to have added Keith Foulke and Curt Schilling in the same offseason," Epstein explained. "We've added two of the best pitchers in baseball. That was one of the weaknesses of our club last year."

The impact of the new pitchers was felt in the first series against the Yankees in April. Battling in Boston, the Red Sox took three of four games, including Schilling's start, and the final game of the series **when Foulke struck out Jason Giambi to earn the save**. Later in April, the Red Sox swept a three-game series from the Yankees in New York. Pedro Martínez threw seven scoreless innings in the series finale, and Francona wisely pulled him for a reliever. The Red Sox went on to win 2–0.

After closing out April with a six-game winning streak, the Red Sox possessed the major leagues' best record at 15-6, but they started May with a five-game losing streak and played .500 baseball for the next two and a half months. Along the way they were swept by the Yankees in New York. In the finale of that series on July 1, **Yankees shortstop Derek Jeter was praised for his phenomenal catch to end the 12th inning, while Red Sox shortstop Nomar Garciaparra was criticized for sitting out the game**. Jeter chased a foul pop off the bat of Trot Nixon into the stands, diving into the seats as he made the catch. He smashed his face into the back of one of the seats and rose with a puffy cheek and the ball in his glove. Runners were on second and third at the time and Jeter went after the ball with reckless abandon. It appeared to be all for naught when Manny Ramírez hit a

> New York Yankees' Derek Jeter dives to catch a fly ball in the twelfth inning against the Boston Red Sox at New York's Yankee Stadium Thursday, July 1, 2004. Jeter left the game and was injured on the play. The Yankees won the game 5–4. AP PHOTO/FRANK FRANKLIN II

go-ahead home run for the Red Sox in the 13th inning, but the Yankees rallied with two runs in the bottom of the inning to win the game, 5–4, and complete the sweep. It was the eighth Boston loss in 11 games and they trailed the Yankees by 8.5 games in the AL East.

"I'm sure it's already an instant classic," Sox outfielder Johnny Damon said. "We still believe we're going to win the World Series. It's never going to be easy in Boston."

Tough times continued the following night in Atlanta when the Red Sox again lost after taking the lead in extra innings. Manny Ramírez singled home the go-ahead run in the 10th inning, but Foulke blew his third save of the year. He gave up a leadoff double to Rafael Furcal, then threw a wild pitch that moved Furcal to third, and allowed the tying run to score on a sacrifice fly off the bat of Braves infielder Nick Green. The Braves went on to win the game, 6–3, when

> Boston Red Sox' Manny Ramirez hits a two-run home run off Texas Rangers' Kenny Rogers in the second inning at Boston's Fenway Park, Saturday, July 10, 2004. AP PHOTO/STEVEN SENNE

Green blasted a three-run homer in the 12th inning off Anastacio Martínez, who had just been called up from the minor leagues that same day. It was Boston's ninth loss in 12 games, and they were just 27-30 since the end of April.

The Red Sox finished the first half of the season winning six of eight games. They completed a sweep of the Oakland A's on July 8 at Fenway Park when Bill Mueller drove home Johnny Damon with a two-out double in the 10th inning. Earlier in the game, David Ortiz broke an 0-for-18 slump with his 23rd home run of the year, and Manny Ramírez hit his 24th.

The Red Sox won their fifth game in a row on July **10 when Ramírez blasted two more home runs against the Texas Rangers.** The Red Sox won 14–6, and had a season-high 21 hits, including five home runs. Garciaparra, still nursing a sore right foot and in the lineup as the designated hitter, continued his hot hitting with a two-run homer. That gave Garciaparra 18 hits in his last 35 at-bats.

The following day the Red Sox wrapped up the first half of the season with a 6–5 loss to the Rangers. The Red Sox went in to the All-Star break with a 48-38 record, seven games behind the Yankees, but one game ahead of the Oakland A's in the wild card race. Manny Ramírez led the American League with 26 home runs, and Ortiz led the league with 78 RBIs. The Red Sox 48 wins were their fewest at the All-Star break in four years, and for the fourth year in a row they were second to the Yankees, but they went into the break with plenty of confidence.

The Red Sox began the second half of the season by losing six of 10 games, including what Johnny Damon called the "worst game we've played all year." Against the worst team in the American League, the Seattle Mariners, a team that was 22 games under .500, the Red Sox took a 4–2 lead into the ninth inning, but Foulke gave up back-to-back solo home runs to Miguel Olivo and Edgar Martínez. It was Foulke's fifth blown save in 19 opportunities. The game went to extra innings when the Red Sox were done in by another Boone. Aaron's brother, Bret, hit an 11th-inning grand slam against Curtis Leskanic. The Red Sox lost, 8–4, and remained seven games behind the Yankees.

On July 23, the Red Sox opened up a three-game series at home against the Yankees. Schilling started the game and gave up seven runs in 5⅓ innings, but Foulke took the loss when he gave up a game-winning double to Alex Rodriguez in the ninth inning. So, despite the fact that Red Sox first baseman **Kevin Millar joined** → **only Lou Gehrig and Mo Vaughn as players to hit three home runs in a Red Sox–Yankees game**, the Red Sox lost, 8–7, and fell 9.5 games behind the Yankees. The two new elite pitchers the Red Sox had acquired did not get the job done, and the

> Boston Red Sox batter Kevin Millar watches the flight of his eighth-inning home run, his third of the game, off New York Yankees pitcher Tom Gordon at Fenway Park in Boston, Friday July 23, 2004. AP PHOTO/CHARLES KRUPA

One Game at a Time

"We didn't dig ourselves a hole too deep to climb out of," Epstein said. "We're very well positioned to get in (the playoffs), if we play good baseball. That's all you can do.**"**

season was not going as planned, and yet here's what Schilling said after the game:

"We were tenacious. We played with intensity. If we play like we played tonight every night for the rest of the season, we're going to go to the World Series."

Schilling was both confident and prescient, and the following night, the Red Sox literally showed how much fight they had in them. **Jason Varitek shoved his glove in the face of Alex Rodriguez,** which incited a brawl, and it was at that moment that the Red Sox began to turn their season around.

> Boston Red Sox catcher Jason Varitek, left, shoves New York Yankees' Alex Rodriguez in the face after Rodriguez was hit by a pitch during the third inning and began yelling at Red Sox pitcher Bronson Arroyo at Fenway Park in Boston Saturday, July 24, 2004. Rodriguez and Varitek were both ejected from the game after the benches cleared. AP PHOTO/WINSLOW TOWNSON

One of the most exciting, dramatic, and important games in Red Sox history almost wasn't played at all. Heavy rains forced a 54-minute delay, and when it looked like the game would be postponed, several Yankees players took showers and prepared to leave. But the Red Sox lobbied for the game to be played. They were ready to go!

With the Red Sox trailing 3–0 in the third inning, Alex Rodriguez was hit by a pitch from Red Sox starter Bronson Arroyo. Rodriguez didn't immediately move toward first base, opting instead to stand and stare at Arroyo. That prompted Red Sox catcher Jason Varitek to jump in front of Rodriguez, and the two of them started shouting at each other. Suddenly, Varitek pushed his catcher's mitt into Rodriguez's face. The benches cleared and several fights took place. Varitek and Rodriguez were ejected along with Sox outfielder Gabe Kapler and Yankees outfielder Kenny Lofton. Order was restored, and the Red Sox scored two in the third and two more in the fourth to take a 4–3 lead. The brawl seemed to inspire the Red Sox, but Arroyo couldn't sustain the momentum. The Yankees scored six times during a sixth inning in which Francona was also ejected for arguing a call at second base. Still fighting, the Red Sox scored four runs in the bottom of the sixth, but trailed 10–8 when they batted in the bottom of the ninth inning. They were three outs away from falling 10.5 games behind the Yankees, and they were facing the great Mariano Rivera, who had converted 23 consecutive save opportunities. The Yankees had won 56 straight games when they held the lead after eight innings. Garciaparra led off the ninth with a double to the gap in left-center field. Millar singled him home. **And Bill Mueller hit a → long flyball into the right field bullpen for a two-run walkoff homer!** The Red Sox won, 11–10.

"I hope we look back a while from now and we're saying that this brought us together," Francona told reporters. "I hope a long time from now we look and say this did it."

› Boston Red Sox' Bill Mueller, right, watches the flight of his game-winning two-run home run in the bottom of the ninth inning as New York Yankees catcher Jorge Posada, left, looks on at Boston's Fenway Park, Saturday, July 24, 2004. The Red Sox beat the Yankees 11–10. AP PHOTO/STEVEN SENNE

Well, if the brawl wasn't the turning point, then it had to be the trade of Nomar Garciaparra a week later. Theo Epstein pulled the trigger on the stunning deal minutes ahead of the trade deadline on July 31. The Red Sox were in Minnesota preparing to battle the Twins. Garciaparra was in the lineup scheduled to bat fifth, and he was already in uniform when Francona pulled him into his office, and handed him the phone. Epstein was on the other end of the line and proceeded to tell the five-time All-Star and two-time batting champion he'd been traded to the Chicago Cubs. Garciaparra was in the final year of his contract and had turned down a four-year, $60 million offer during the offseason. He had also missed the first 57 games of the season with Achilles' tendinitis, and was likely to miss many more games during the remainder of the season because of the injury. So, Epstein made the four-team, eight-player blockbuster deal, and the Red Sox ended up with two Gold Glove infielders, shortstop Orlando Cabrera from the Expos and first baseman Doug Mientkiewicz from the Twins. In a separate deal the Red Sox

▶ Boston Red Sox' Pedro Martinez, second from right, celebrates his ninth-inning shutout of the Tampa Bay Devil Rays with catcher Jason Varitek, right, Thursday, Aug. 12, 2004, in Boston. Boston won, 6–0. AP PHOTO/MICHAEL DWYER

sent minor-league outfielder Henri Stanley to the Los Angeles Dodgers in exchange for speedy veteran outfielder Dave Roberts.

"I thought there was a flaw on the club that we couldn't allow to become a fatal flaw," Epstein explained. "That the defense on this team is not championship caliber. In my mind we were not going to win a World Series with our defense the way it was."

Once the deal was announced, Garciaparra changed into his street clothes, said his good-byes, and left the ballpark. Mientkiewicz took off his Twins uniform, walked across to the Red Sox clubhouse, and put on his new Red Sox uniform. He started for the Red Sox at first base and had two hits and scored a run, but the Red Sox lost, 5–4, when Jacque Jones hit a solo home run off Alan Embree in the eighth inning.

The Red Sox went just 8-7 in the first 15 games after the trade. **During the stretch, Pedro Martínez pitched his first shutout in nearly four years** with a 10-strikeout performance against the Tampa Bay Rays, but after a 5–4 loss to the Chicago White Sox on August 15, the Red Sox were 10.5 games behind the Yankees, and had fallen into a tie with the Rangers in the wild card race. However, from that point on, the Red Sox played amazing baseball! They won 16 of their next 17 games, and 20 of their next 22.

On August 17, **Cabrera, who was just 13-for-62 since coming to Boston, doubled home the game-winning run** to beat the Toronto Blue Jays at Fenway Park. Three days later, Cabrera homered and drove in four runs as Schilling won his 15th game, and the Red Sox beat the White Sox, 10–1. The Red Sox extended

> Boston Red Sox' Orlando Cabrera is mobbed by teammates at third base after his game-winning hit in the bottom of the ninth inning of a 5–4 win over the Toronto Blue Jays at Fenway Park in Boston Tuesday, Aug. 17, 2004. AP PHOTO/WINSLOW TOWNSON

their winning streak to six games on August 22, when Ramírez and Ortiz hit back-to-back home runs in the eighth inning to beat the White Sox, 6–5.

The next day, Blue Jays left-hander Ted Lilly threw a three-hit shutout against the Red Sox, but the Red Sox responded by winning their next 10 games. By the end of the streak, the Red Sox were just 2.5 games behind the Yankees, and held a 4.5-game lead in the wild card race over Anaheim. On September 5, Schilling won his league-leading 18th game, 6–5, against the Texas Rangers. Schilling pitched into the ninth inning, and for the fifth straight game, didn't walk a batter. The win completed a 9-1 homestand for the Red Sox.

"We played such good baseball in every aspect," Schilling said. "I just feel like we are such a good team right now that we can win with pitching, hitting, defense, bullpen . . . whatever you need to do on a given night to win. And that's what championship teams do."

Three days later, Martinez improved his record to 16-5 when he threw six scoreless innings at the Oakland A's. It was his 117th win for the Red Sox, tying him with Smoky Joe Wood for fifth place in team history. The Red Sox were 30 games over .500, and only two games behind the Yankees. The Red Sox won four of their next seven games, but lost more ground to the Yankees. So, they were 3.5 games behind their rivals when they arrived in New York on September 17 to begin a three-game series.

The Yankees took a 2–1 lead to the ninth inning in the series opener and gave the ball to Mariano Rivera, who was looking to tie his career high with his 50th save. Trot Nixon led off the Red Sox ninth with a walk, and was lifted for pinch-runner Dave

> Boston Red Sox Johnny Damon hits a single to drive in the winning run in the ninth inning against the New York Yankees Friday night, Sept. 17, 2004, at Yankee Stadium in New York. The Red Sox came from behind to beat the Yankees, 3–2. AP PHOTO/BILL KOSTROUN

Roberts, who stole second. After Kevin Millar was hit by a pitch, Orlando Cabrera singled to score Roberts. **Millar moved to second on the base hit and scored when Johnny Damon looped a soft single that landed just in front of Yankees outfielder Kenny Lofton.** Keith Foulke pitched a perfect ninth for his 30th save in 35 chances, and the Red Sox won, 3–2. They now trailed the Yankees by 2.5 games, and once again proved they weren't intimidated by the best closer in the game.

The Yankees responded the next day by knocking Sox starter Derek Lowe out of the game in the second inning of a 14–4 rout, and the Yankees won the series finale when they scored eight runs against Pedro Martínez. The Red Sox were soundly beaten 25–5 in the last two games, and left New York 4.5 games behind the Yankees.

The Red Sox returned home, where two walkoff victories helped them split a four-game series with the Baltimore Orioles. In the second game of the series, Schilling threw eight shutout innings, but was locked in a pitchers' duel with Rodrigo López. The only Red Sox run came in the eighth inning, when Johnny Damon scored on a Kevin Millar sacrifice fly. Foulke was called upon to protect a 1–0 lead, but blew the save when he gave up a single to Miguel Tejada and a two-strike, two-run homer to Javy López. Having lost the final two games against the Yankees,

and the opener to the Orioles, the Red Sox were in danger of losing a fourth straight game. But the Red Sox rallied in the ninth. With two outs and runners on second and third, **Mark Bellhorn, who** → **would lead the league in strikeouts and establish a Red Sox franchise record for strikeouts with 177, delivered a game-winning double to the wall in center field**. The Red Sox won, 3–2, and they'd walk off with another win the next night!

David Ortiz hit his 40th home run in the seventh inning to give

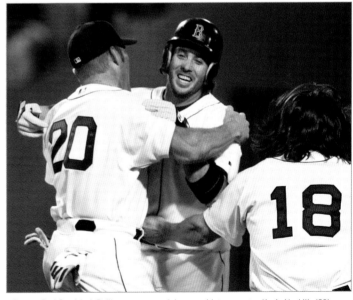

> Boston Red Sox Mark Bellhorn, center, celebrates with teammates Kevin Youkilis (20) and Johnny Damon (18) after his game-winning single drove in two runs in the ninth inning against the Baltimore Orioles at Fenway Park in Boston Tuesday, Sept. 21, 2004. The Red Sox came from behind to win, 3–2. AP PHOTO/ELISE AMENDOLA

> Boston Red Sox' Orlando Cabrera, right, throws off his helmet as he is met at home plate by teammates Pedro Martinez, center, and Manny Ramirez (24) after his walkoff home run in the bottom of the 12th inning against the Baltimore Orioles at Fenway Park in Boston, Wednesday Sept. 22, 2004. The Red Sox won 7–6. AP PHOTO/CHARLES KRUPA

the Red Sox a 6–5 lead, and that score held until the ninth inning when Foulke blew his seventh game of the year. Five of those blown saves occurred at Fenway Park, but the Red Sox went on to win all five of those games. This one lasted until **Cabrera led off the 12th inning with his fifth home run of the year**, his first since joining the Red Sox.

The Red Sox lost the series finale to Baltimore, and then welcomed the Yankees into town. Only 10 games remained in the season and the Red Sox trailed the Yankees by 4.5 games. The Red Sox needed a sweep to have any chance of preventing the Yankees from winning a seventh straight American League East division title. In the series opener, Pedro Martínez pitched seven strong innings, and the Red Sox led 4–3, but inexplicably, Terry Francona made the same mistake that cost Grady Little his job. Francona sent Martínez back out to the mound for the eighth inning. Martínez had already thrown 101 pitches, and on his 103rd, **Hideki Matsui hit his first and only home run ever against Martínez**. Bernie Williams followed with a ground-rule double, and Ruben Sierra eventually drove home the go-ahead run with a single that knocked Martínez out of the game. The Red Sox went on to lose, 6–4.

> Boston Red Sox pitcher Pedro Martinez reacts to giving up an RBI single to New York Yankees' Ruben Sierra in the eighth inning against the New York Yankees, Friday, Sept. 24, 2004, in Boston. AP PHOTO/WINSLOW TOWNSON

> New York Yankees' Derek Jeter, right, congratulates teammate Hideki Matsui after Matsui's solo home run off Boston Red Sox starter Pedro Martinez during the eighth inning Friday, Sept. 24, 2004, in Boston. AP PHOTO/WINSLOW TOWNSON

"What can I say," Martínez famously said after the game, "Just tip my hat and call the Yankees my daddy. I can't find a way to beat them at this point. They're that good. They're that hot right now—at least against me. I wish they would disappear and not come back."

The Red Sox won the final two games of the series, including their final home game of the season when once again high tension led to a bench-clearing incident. Red Sox reliever Pedro Astacio threw a pitch behind Kenny Lofton in the eighth inning, and both teams received a warning from the home-plate umpire. The warning did no good, however, as Yankee reliever Brad Halsey went up and in with a pitch to Dave Roberts in the bottom of the inning. Both benches and bullpens emptied onto the field, but players were kept under control. The Red Sox won, 11–4, as Schilling picked up his 21st and final win of the year. The Red Sox won 11 of the 19 games against the Yankees, taking the season series against them for the first time in five years. The game also marked the 45th game the Red Sox and Yankees had played against one another, including the playoffs, since the start of the 2003 season. And they weren't done yet!

The Red Sox still had seven road games left in the season, and they clinched a playoff berth the next night in Tampa with a 7–3 win over the Rays. The win secured at least the wild card. They followed that with another dramatic victory in their last at-bat when Kevin Millar hit a two-out, two-run homer in the 11th inning. The Red Sox won 10–8, and still had hopes of overtaking the Yankees in the division race. Those aspirations ended when the Yankees won their 100th game on September 30, and relegated the Red Sox to their seventh straight second-place finish. The Red Sox finished with 98 wins, three games behind the Yankees, but with the best record in all of baseball (42-19) after the trade of Garciaparra. They would head into the postseason as the hottest team in baseball. Their 949 runs scored were the most in baseball. And their dominating pair of aces, Schilling and Martínez, would finish second and fourth, respectively, in the Cy Young balloting. In short, the Red Sox were ready! And according to Johnny Damon, they were no longer the "Cowboy Up" Red Sox of 2003. They were idiots!

"We're just the idiots this year," Damon announced before the start of the playoffs. "We were just a bunch of cowboys out there last year, just enjoying every minute. Now we know we have something to prove. We don't want to be remembered as a team that, okay, we keep making it to the playoffs, but we keep having tough losses. I mean, we want to be known as a team that rewrites history books."

The Red Sox began the postseason in Anaheim taking on the Angels in the divisional round. In Game 1, Schilling pitched 6⅔ effective innings, Ramírez and Millar homered during a seven-run fourth inning, and the Red Sox went on to win, 9–3. In Game 2, Pedro Martínez, who posted a 7.72 ERA while losing his last four starts of the regular season, threw seven strong innings. Jason Varitek homered, and the Red Sox won, 8–3. **The Red Sox came home to complete the sweep when David Ortiz hit a 10th-inning, two-run, game-winning, series-clinching walkoff home run!** The Red Sox won, 8–6, and found out a day later that they'd be facing the Yankees in the American League Championship Series for the second year in a row. The Red Sox got there by outscoring the Angels, 25–12, while the Yankees advanced by squeaking past the Minnesota Twins in four games, including two wins in extra innings. Alex Rodriguez scored the series-clinching run when he raced home on a wild pitch in the 11th inning of Game 4. Mariano Rivera closed out the game, and the Yankees prepared for an ALCS rematch against the fearless foes of Boston.

"This is what everybody drew up in spring training," Yankees slugger Gary Sheffield told reporters. "Now everybody gets to see what it's all about. When Schilling went to the Red Sox, and when A-Rod came here, that's what everybody wanted to see."

Just as they had done for the series against the Angels, the Red Sox gave the ball to Schilling for Game 1. After all, his 21 wins made him the team's ace. He was 6-1 with a 1.74 ERA in 12

> Boston Red Sox teammates watch David Ortiz's (34) homer in the 10th inning in Boston Friday, Oct. 8, 2004. The Sox defeated the Angels 8–6 to sweep the AL Division Series. AP PHOTO/WINSLOW TOWNSON

career playoff starts, and he was brought to the Red Sox for the specific purpose of helping them get past the Yankees and win a World Series.

"I'm not sure I can think of any scenario more enjoyable than making 55,000 people from New York shut up," Schilling said before the series got underway.

But Schilling had injured a tendon in his right ankle in September, and tweaked it in his start against the Twins. He was injected with a painkiller before his Game 1 start against the Yankees in New York, and then went out and gave up six runs in three innings.

"If I can't go out there with something better than that," he said, "I'm not going back out there."

The Red Sox fell behind 8–0, and didn't put a baserunner on against Yankees starter Mike Mussina until the seventh inning. Bellhorn broke up Mussina's bid for a perfect game with a one-out double. That opened the floodgates as the Red Sox scored five runs in the seventh, and two more in the eighth. Jason Varitek's two-run homer in the seventh was his franchise-best eighth postseason home run, one more than Garciaparra. And when David Ortiz tripled home two runs with two outs in the eighth inning off Yankees setup man Tom Gordon, the Red Sox trailed 8–7, and Ortiz stood on third base representing the tying run. However, Rivera entered the game and induced Kevin Millar to pop up to end the threat. Rivera had only arrived at Yankee Stadium in the second inning, because he had flown back to Panama for the funeral of two of his relatives who had been electrocuted in the swimming pool of his home. Despite his heavy heart, Rivera got the final three outs and picked up his 31st career postseason save. The Red Sox lost the opener, 10–7.

The Yankees took a commanding 2–0 lead in the series when Pedro Martínez was outpitched by Yankees veteran Jon Lieber in Game 2. Martínez gave up a run in the first and a two-run homer to John Olerud in the sixth while Lieber carried a shutout into the eighth inning, and the Yankees went on to win, 3–1. During the game, Yankees fans serenaded Martínez with long, loud chants of "Who's your Daddy?", which Martinez said didn't bother him at all.

"It actually made me feel really, really good," he reasoned. "I actually realized that I was somebody important because I got the atten-tion of 60,000 people. Fifteen years ago, I was sitting under a mango tree without 50 cents to actually pay for a bus, and today, I was the center of attention of the whole city of New York. I thank God for that."

Game 3 was scheduled for Friday, October 15 at Fenway Park, but was postponed due to rain and played the following night instead. Neither starting pitcher made it out of the third inning. The Yankees got the hit parade started with three runs off Bronson Arroyo in the first inning. The Red Sox responded with four runs off Kevin Brown in the second. Alex Rodriguez, who helped ignite a brawl when he was hit by an Arroyo pitch in July, gained some measure of revenge when he led off the third with a home run to tie the game, 4–4. The Yankees took the lead by adding two more runs in the inning. Brown was relieved by Javier Vázquez to start the Red Sox half of the third inning. Vázquez loaded the bases with one out, and Orlando Cabrera hit a line shot to the gap in

> Boston Red Sox' Bill Mueller hits an RBI single in the ninth inning to tie the game against the New York Yankees in Game 4 of the ALCS Sunday, Oct. 17, 2004, in Boston.
AP PHOTO/CHARLES KRUPA

deep right field. Two runs scored, but Mueller was thrown out at the plate, and Damon grounded out to end the threat. The game was tied 6–6 after three innings, but the Yankees scored the next 11 runs, pounding five different Red Sox relievers along the way. No one was spared! In the end, the teams combined for a League Championship Series record 27 runs, and the Yankees scored 19 of them. Sheffield, Matsui, and Rodriguez combined to go 12-for-16 with five doubles, four home runs, and 12 RBIs. At four hours and 20 minutes, the game was the longest nine-inning contest in postseason history.

The Red Sox were down 3–0 in the series, and up to that point, no major-league team had ever won a best-of-seven series in which they had lost the first three games. In fact, 20 of the 25 teams that had fallen into a 3–0 hole were swept in four straight. The Red Sox remained full of confidence. Instead of feeling the pressure of not having won a World Series in 86 years, the Red Sox put the pressure squarely on the broad shoulders of the Yankees.

"Don't let us win tonight," Millar stated before Game 4. "This is a big game. They've got to win, because if we win we've got Pedro coming back, and then Schilling will pitch Game 6, and then you can take that fraud stuff and put it to — bed. Don't let the Sox win this game."

Red Sox fans will always remember Game 4 for three big moments: (1) Dave Roberts's ninth-inning stolen base; (2) Bill Mueller's single that tied the game; and (3) David Ortiz's 12th-inning home run that won it. But a lot more happened during the five hours and two minutes that the Red Sox and Yankees played tension-filled baseball at Fenway Park.

> Boston Red Sox' David Ortiz celebrates after hitting the game-winning homer in the bottom of the 12th to defeat the New York Yankees 6–4 during Game 4 of the ALCS Sunday, Oct. 17, 2004, in Boston. AP PHOTO/CHARLES KRUPA

Taking It One at a Time

David Ortiz finished his Red Sox career with 20 walk-off hits, including three in the postseason. He also had 3 walk-off hits with the Minnesota Twins before coming to Boston.

The game began with Red Sox right-hander Derek Lowe on the mound. Despite winning 14 games in the regular season as a starter, Lowe had been pushed out of the starting rotation and into the bullpen for the postseason. Francona made the decision because Lowe had given up 18 runs in 10⅓ innings over his last four starts, which included the worst start of his career just one month earlier at Yankee Stadium. The fading hopes of Red Sox Nation rested with Lowe, who had given up seven runs in one inning-plus of work the last time he had faced the Yankees. But Francona had no choice. Tim Wakefield, originally slated to start Game 4, gave up the chance to start when he volunteered to save the bullpen in Game 3 and wound up throwing 3⅓ innings.

Lowe retired the Yankees in order in the first inning, and escaped the second when Hideki Matsui was thrown out at the plate trying to score from third on a groundball to Orlando Cabrera at shortstop. That would prove to be a huge play in a game that would go to extra innings. Lowe surrendered a two-run homer to Alex Rodriguez in the third, and the Yankees took a 2–0 lead into the fifth inning. That's when the Red Sox scored three times, two runs coming home on Ortiz's big two-out bases-loaded single to give the Red Sox the lead.

After Lowe gave up a one-out triple to Matsui in the sixth, he was relieved by Mike Timlin. The Yankees didn't get a ball out of the infield against Timlin, but a walk and three infield hits produced two runs. The Yankees had a chance to blow the game wide open, but Timlin got Derek Jeter to ground out with the bases loaded to end the threat. The Yankees held a 4–3 lead, and it stayed that way until the bottom of the ninth. The Red Sox were three outs away from being swept by their archrivals!

Mariano Rivera was back in a familiar position. He had a record 32 postseason saves with only four blown opportunities, but the Red Sox knew they could get to him. Bill Mueller's two-run homer on July 24 to beat Rivera and the Yankees was still fresh on the minds of the Red Sox and their fans. And then it happened again!

Kevin Millar led off with a walk, and Dave Roberts was inserted as a pinch-runner. Everybody knew Roberts would try to steal second. He was 38-for-41 in stolen base attempts during the regular season. Rivera threw over to first three times, and then on the first pitch to Mueller, Roberts took off. Yankees catcher Jorge Posada's throw was right on the money, but Roberts dove headfirst and got his left hand to the base before Jeter's sweep tag. The tying run was on second! Two pitches later, Mueller laced a single back up the middle and into center field. Roberts raced around third base, and scored the tying run. The winning run was now on first with nobody out. Pinch-hitter Doug Mientkiewicz bunted Mueller to second. Damon reached on an error by Yankee first baseman Tony Clark, and after Cabrera struck out, Manny Ramírez walked to load the bases. David Ortiz stepped to the plate, but his game-winning dramatics would have to wait. Big Papi popped up to second to end the inning.

Curtis Leskanic was not the likeliest of candidates to earn the victory in one of the most important games in Red Sox history. He had been released by the Kansas City Royals in June, and signed by the Red Sox to a minor-league contract, yet there he was, called upon with two outs and the bases loaded in the 11th inning, charged with the responsibility of retiring five-time All-Star Bernie Williams. If he failed, the long run of frustration for the Red Sox would continue, but Leskanic got Williams to flyout to center, and after the Red Sox failed to score in their half of the inning, Leskanic was back out on the hill for the top of the 12th. After surrendering a leadoff single to Posada, Leskanic retired the next three Yankees. He struck out Miguel Cairo to end the inning, and it was the last pitch of Leskanic's career.

> Boston Red Sox' Johnny Damon is mobbed by teammates after he scored the winning run against the New York Yankees on David Ortiz's single in the 14th inning during Game 5 of the ALCS Monday, Oct. 18, 2004, in Boston. The Red Sox won, 5–4.
AP PHOTO/ELISE AMENDOLA

The 36-year-old wasn't used again during the playoffs, and retired at the end of the season.

After getting two perfect innings from Tom Gordon, the Yankees went to Paul Quantrill in the 12th. He gave up a leadoff single to Manny Ramírez, and a walkoff two-run homer to David Ortiz!

"Ortiz into deep right field. Back is Sheffield," FOX-TV announcer Joe Buck said making the call, and then as the ball landed over the wall, "We'll see you later tonight!"

The Red Sox survived with a 6–4 victory, but they still had a long way to go in their marathon day. Game 4 ended at 1:22 a.m. and Game 5 would start less than 16 hours later. It would last 14 innings, and take five hours, 49 minutes to determine a winner. **Once again, David Ortiz would be at the center of it all.** He began with a first-inning RBI single, added an eighth-inning home run, and then amazed baseball fans everywhere with his third walkoff hit of the postseason—a two-out single in the 14th inning to score Johnny Damon. Ortiz's heroics made it the most incredible 24 hours for any player in baseball history!

The Red Sox led 2–1 in the sixth inning with Pedro Martínez outdueling the Yankees' ace Mike Mussina, but Martínez gave up a three-run double to Derek Jeter, and the Red Sox suddenly trailed 4–2. In the eighth, Ortiz led off with a home run off Tom Gordon, and after the Red Sox put runners on first and third with nobody out, Varitek hit a sacrifice fly off Rivera to tie the game.

The Red Sox bullpen took over from there, striking out 10 hitters over eight shutout innings. Keith Foulke, who had thrown 50 pitches over 2⅓ innings in Game 4, threw another 20 pitches to record four outs in Game 5, and Wakefield pitched the final three innings to pick up the win.

"The last two nights shows the depth, the character, the heart, the guts of our ball club," Wakefield said. "It took every ounce of whatever we had left to win tonight's game and to win last night's game."

Ortiz won it with a two-out, 10-pitch at-bat in the 14th inning. His bloop single against Esteban Loaiza into center field easily scored Damon from second base, and the Red Sox won, 5–4. A second straight come-from-behind walkoff victory!

The series moved back down to Yankee Stadium for Game 6, where **Schilling would get a second chance to make 55,000 Yankees fans shut up, but first there was the serious matter of the torn tendon in his right ankle.** Needing to stabilize the tendon, Red Sox team doctors came up with the idea of sewing the tendon with skin from Schilling's leg, and creating a wall of stitches to keep the tendon from slipping out of place. Dr. Bill Morgan first practiced on a cadaver, and then on the Monday afternoon of Game 5, he sewed three stitches into Schilling's

> Boston Red Sox pitcher Curt Schilling tends to his right ankle during the third inning of Game 6 of the ALCS against the New York Yankees in this file photo taken on Tuesday, Oct. 19, 2004, in New York. Baltimore Orioles broadcaster Gary Thorne said Wednesday night, April 25, 2007, that Schilling painted the sock red as a public relations stunt in the Red Sox Game 6 win over the Yankees in the 2004 American League Championship Series. AP PHOTO/CHARLES KRUPA

> New York Yankees' Alex Rodriguez knocks the ball out of the glove of Boston Red Sox pitcher Bronson Arroyo, left, as first baseman Doug Mientkiewicz looks on during the eighth inning of Game 6 of the ALCS in New York, Tuesday, Oct. 19, 2004. Rodriguez was initially called safe, but after conferring, the umpires ruled he was out for interference. AP PHOTO/AMY SANCETTA

ankle. Schilling flew to New York and pitched seven innings the next day. With blood staining his sock, he allowed just one run on four hits.

The game also featured two calls reversed by the umpires in favor of the Red Sox. First, Mark Bellhorn's fourth-inning blast off Jon Lieber, originally called a ground-rule double, was changed to a three-run homer, and the Red Sox took a 4–0 lead.

Later, Bernie Williams homered off Schilling in the seventh to cut the Red Sox lead to 4–1, and after Derek Jeter singled home a run off Bronson Arroyo in the eighth, it was a 4–2 game with Alex Rodriguez stepping up to the plate representing the tying run. Rodriguez hit a slow roller down the first-base line. **Arroyo fielded the ball and attempted to tag Rodriguez, but Rodriguez slapped Arroyo's glove and knocked the ball free.** As the ball rolled into right field, Jeter came all the way around to score from first, and Rodriguez raced to second base. Francona came out to argue, and the umpires again correctly changed the call. They called Rodriguez out for intentionally swatting Arroyo's glove

> Boston Red Sox' Johnny Damon, left, hits a second-inning grand slam home run against the New York Yankees in Game 7 of the ALCS in New York, Wednesday, Oct. 20, 2004, off relief pitcher Javier Vazquez. Jorge Posada catches for the Yankees and umpire Randy Marsh officiates. AP PHOTO/BILL KOSTROUN

with his left hand, and Jeter was sent back to first base. The game was delayed further when fans threw trash on the field in protest. Foulke pitched a scoreless ninth, striking out Tony Clark on a 3–2 pitch with two runners on to secure the 4–2 win, and force an ALCS Game 7 between the Red Sox and Yankees for a second straight year!

As soon as Schilling was lifted from the game, his stitches were removed, and he appeared at the postgame news conference wearing a T-shirt with the phrase, "Why not us?" And considering the Red Sox were humiliated in Game 3, and then survived with 26 innings, and nearly 11 hours of baseball in Games 4 and 5, and they had already done what no other team had done by forcing a Game 7 after losing the first three games—anything was possible! Including a Game 7 blowout!

David Ortiz, who finished with three home runs and 11 RBIs on his way to being named Series MVP, hit a two-run homer off Kevin Brown in the first inning. **Damon hit a grand slam into the front row of the right field bleachers off Javier Vázquez in the second**, and added a two-run shot in the fourth. The outcome was never in doubt. Derek Lowe, pitching on two days' rest, gave up one run in six innings, and the Red Sox completed the greatest comeback in baseball history with a 10–3 victory! The Red Sox rushed the field and celebrated where they had suffered so many disappointments, including their own collapse just a year earlier.

"This one is for all those great Red Sox players and teams who would have been in the World Series were it not for the Yankees," Epstein said. "It's for 1949, '78, '03. It's all for them. I hope Ted Williams is having a cocktail upstairs! Now we start worrying about how to win four more games and really do something that's been a long time coming for this franchise."

▶ Boston Red Sox' Mark Bellhorn hits an eighth-inning two-run home run off St. Louis Cardinals' Julian Tavarez in Game 1 of the World Series in Boston, Saturday, Oct. 23, 2004. AP PHOTO/CHARLES KRUPA

The 2004 World Series began on Saturday, October 23, at Fenway Park. The Red Sox played host to the St. Louis Cardinals, who had beaten Roger Clemens and the Houston Astros in Game 7 of the National League Championship Series. The Cardinals won a major-league best 105 games during the regular season, and were expected to be a formidable opponent, but the Red Sox swept them in four games!

In Game 1, Ortiz got things started with a three-run homer in the first inning off Cardinals right-hander Woody Williams. The Red Sox would grab a 7–2 lead in the third inning when Manny Ramírez, who didn't have an RBI in the ALCS, hit a run-scoring groundout. The Cardinals rallied back to tie the game 7–7 in the sixth inning when Larry Walker's fourth hit of the game scored Edgar Rentería. The Red Sox would retake the lead before Ramírez made errors on consecutive plays in the eighth inning. First, he bobbled a base hit by Rentería, allowing one run to score, and then he tried to make a sliding catch on a flyball off the bat of Walker, but the ball bounced off his glove, allowing another run to score, and the game was again tied, 9–9. In the eighth inning, **Mark Bellhorn homered for a third straight game**, this one clanging off the Pesky Pole in right, a two-run shot that lifted the Red Sox to an 11–9 victory.

Curt Schilling had the stitches put back in to stabilize his right ankle tendon before Game 2, and then threw six effective innings, allowing just one run. The Red Sox got a two-run triple from Varitek in the first, a two-run double from Bellhorn in the fourth, and a two-run single from Orlando Cabrera in the sixth. The Red Sox committed four errors for the second straight game, but won easily, 6–2, and headed for St. Louis with a 2–0 lead in the series.

Pedro Martínez pitched seven scoreless innings to win Game 3, getting help from Manny Ramírez, who homered in the first inning, and then threw Larry Walker out at the plate to end the Cardinals' half of the inning. With the Red Sox leading 1–0 in the third, the Cardinals put runners on second and third with nobody out. The Red Sox played their infield back, willing to concede a run, and it looked as if that's what they had done when Walker grounded to second

> In this Oct. 27, 2004, file photo, Boston Red Sox catcher Jason Varitek leaps into the arms of pitcher Keith Foulke (29) after the Red Sox beat the St. Louis Cardinals 3–0 to sweep the World Series, in St. Louis. Now that the news was out Varitek decided to retire after 15 seasons as the catcher in Boston, it doesn't make it any easier to take. AP PHOTO/SUE OGROCKI

> Boston Red Sox pitcher Pedro Martinez holds up the championship trophy after the Red Sox defeated the St. Louis Cardinals 3–0 in Game 4 to win the World Series at Busch Stadium in St. Louis, Wednesday, Oct. 27, 2004. AP PHOTO/SUE OGROCKI

base. Bellhorn threw to first for the out, but the runner on third, starting pitcher Jeff Suppan, started home and then stopped. Ortiz, playing first base for the first time in months, threw to third where Mueller tagged Suppan out. Instead of tying the game, the Cardinals ran themselves into a double play. Martínez retired the final 14 batters he faced and the Red Sox won, 4–1. It was the last game Martínez ever pitched for the Red Sox. He would sign a free agent contract with the New York Mets during the offseason.

Game 4 was a coronation! Like Martínez before him, Derek Lowe pitched seven scoreless innings. Johnny Damon slammed the fourth pitch of the game over the wall in right-center, and Trot Nixon added a two-run double in the third. **The Red Sox never trailed in the series and completed the sweep with a tension-free 3–0 win.** Keith Foulke closed out all four World Series games, finishing a spectacular postseason with just one run allowed in 14 innings.

Following their 19–8 loss to the Yankees in Game 3 of the ALCS, the Red Sox won eight straight games in 11 days, and successfully buried 86 years of frustration. An estimated three million people lined the streets for Boston's third duck boat parade in less than three years, and there would be another one three months later!

Radio Waves

"Swing, and a groundball stabbed by Foulke," longtime Red Sox radio voice Joe Castiglione began his call of the final out. "He has it. He underhands to first, and the Boston Red Sox are World Champions! For the first time in 86 years, the Red Sox have won baseball's world championship. Can you believe it?"

> The grave of George Herman "Babe" Ruth is decorated with items left by New York Yankees and Boston Red Sox fans, Thursday, Oct. 28, 2004, in Hawthorne. The "Curse of the Bambino" has followed Boston through four World Series defeats, each one in seven games. The end of the drought came Wednesday, Oct. 27, when Boston completed a sweep of the St. Louis Cardinals to win the World Series. AP PHOTO/MARY ALTAFFER

CHAPTER FOUR

THE
2004 NEW ENGLAND PATRIOTS

Owner:
Robert Kraft

Vice President of Player Personnel:
Scott Pioli

Head Coach:
Bill Belichick

Regular Season Record:
14-2

Regular Season Finish:
AFC East Champions

Playoff Results:
Divisional Round—New England Patriots 20
Indianapolis Colts 3

AFC Championship—New England Patriots 41
Pittsburgh Steelers 27

Super Bowl:
New England Patriots 24
Philadelphia Eagles 21

Awards:
Super Bowl MVP: WR Deion Branch

Pro Bowlers: QB Tom Brady, LB Tedy Bruschi,
RB Corey Dillon, SpT Larry Izzo, DT Richard
Seymour, K Adam Vinatieri

T he Patriots finished the 2003 season on a 12-game winning streak, then rolled through the playoffs with three more wins, including their second Super Bowl title in three years—and then they got better! They began by releasing running back Antowain Smith. Smith had rushed for 83 yards on 26 carries in the Super Bowl victory over Carolina, but the Patriots saw him as a player in decline. The Patriots significantly upgraded the position on April 19, 2004, when they acquired three-time Pro Bowl running back Corey Dillon from the Cincinnati Bengals. The 29-year-old Dillon had rushed for more than 1,100 yards in each of his first six NFL seasons, but frequently complained in public that he didn't get the ball enough, and that he was tired of being on a losing team. Early in the 2003 season, he announced he wanted to be traded. His seventh and final season with the Bengals was his least productive. He battled a groin injury and lost his starting job, and as he walked off the field after the last game of the season, he threw his helmet, shoulder pads, and cleats into the stands. He did not seem to be a perfect fit for the Patriots! But the Patriots acquired him for a second-round draft choice, and

convinced him to lower his base salaries for the final two years of his contract. The Patriots determined he was worth the risk, and their gamble paid off.

Five days after the Dillon trade, the NFL Draft was held, and the Patriots were pleasantly surprised to see big Vince Wilfork still available when it was their turn to pick at number 21 in the first round. **They grabbed the 330-pound nose tackle from the University of Miami and stuck him in the middle of their defensive line for the next 11 years.**

The Patriots were ready to defend their Super Bowl title, but first, there was the little matter of cornerback Ty Law repeatedly calling Bill Belichick a liar in public. Law's contention was that the Patriots agreed to negotiate a new contract with him, but when negotiations stalled, the Patriots decided to stop the talks and just pay Law his $7 million salary for 2004. Law considered the Patriots backing away from negotiations a lie, and voiced his displeasure first to the *Boston Globe*.

"Right now, it's not about money," Law told the newspaper in March. "That bridge is burned. I no longer want to be a Patriot. I can't even see myself putting on that uniform again, that's how bad I feel about playing here."

Law actually had two years and $17 million left on his contract, but as a four-time Pro Bowl selection, and now 30 years old, Law wanted to be the highest-paid cornerback in football. Still, there wasn't much he could do about his situation other than to hold out, and he wasn't about to do that, because his contract called for a million-dollar bonus just for showing up to training camp on time.

"It's not a reason to hold out," Law continued. "I get one million just to show up. Who wouldn't show up for a million? The money ain't the thing, because I have that. Then again, I'm not going to sit here and say I don't want 7 million, either. That's stupid. Hell, we all gotta eat."

Law's offseason also included an April arrest in Miami Beach when he was pulled over in his Rolls-Royce for a lane violation. Law initially sped away, and was stopped a second time, and then ran on foot from police before being caught

> New England Patriots linebacker Willie McGinest (55) wraps up Indianapolis Colts quarterback Peyton Manning for a sack late in the fourth quarter at Gillette Stadium in Foxborough, Mass. Thursday, Sept. 9, 2004. The Patriots defeated the Colts, 27–24, in the NFL season opener.
AP PHOTO/ELISE AMENDOLA

and arrested. Charges of disobeying a lawful command and resisting arrest were dropped later that summer, and Law began the 2004 NFL season without a new contract, but on the field as the Patriots beat the Colts, 27–24, at Gillette Stadium.

It was another nail-biter between the Patriots and Colts. The Patriots defense looked terrible giving up 202 yards rushing, but it made two big plays in the fourth quarter to secure the victory. First, with under four minutes to play and the Patriots clinging to a 27–24 lead, Patriot cornerback Tyrone Poole was called for pass interference in the end zone, giving the Colts first-and-goal at the 1-yard line. Colts running back Edgerrin James, who had run so effectively throughout the game, but who had already fumbled the ball away once, did so again. Instead of rushing in for the go-ahead touchdown, James had the ball stripped away by Patriots safety Eugene Wilson.

Rookie Vince Wilfork fell on top of the ball, and it looked like the Patriot victory was secured. However, the Patriots were forced to punt, giving the Colts one final chance with 1:54 remaining. The Colts drive started at their own 36, but the first play was a 45-yard completion from Manning to Brandon Stokley. The Colts got the ball to the Patriots' 17-yard line, and were quickly in range for placekicker Mike Vanderjagt, who had made 42 consecutive field goals. On third-and-8, **McGinest sacked Manning for a 12-yard loss**, pushing the ball back to the 29-yard line.

"It seems that Willie always seems to be there when we need him," Belichick said.

Now confronted with a 47-yard field goal attempt instead of a chip shot, Vanderjagt missed! The Patriots ran out the clock and won the season opener. Tom Brady had touchdown passes to Deion Branch, David Patten, and Daniel Graham, and running back Corey Dillon ran for 86 yards as the Patriots won their 16th game in a row.

The next victims were the Arizona Cardinals. The Patriots defense came up with five sacks and a pair of Eugene Wilson interceptions. **Corey Dillon ran for 158 yards, and Brady found Daniel Graham for two more touchdown passes.** The Patriots won 23–12. Their winning streak was up to 17 games, one shy of the NFL record.

"What streak?" Belichick said. "We're just trying to win a game."

Taking It One Yard at a Time

Only 13 running backs have ever rushed for over 1,000 yards in a single season with the Patriots. None ran for more than Corey Dillon's 1,635 yards in 2004.

▸ New England Patriots running back Corey Dillon (28) scrambles past Arizona Cardinals James Darling during the fourth quarter Sunday, Sept. 19, 2004, at Sun Devil Stadium in Tempe, Ariz. The Patriots won 23–12. AP PHOTO/RICK HOSSMAN

> Buffalo Bills quarterback Drew Bledsoe, right, looks to pass to Bills' Mark Cambell (84), while under pressure from New England Patriots' Mike Vrabel, center, in the first half Sunday, Oct. 3, 2004, in Orchard Park, N.Y. The Patriots won, 31–17. AP PHOTO/DAVID DUPREY

But the Patriots hadn't lost a game in a full calendar year, and following their bye week, they were back in Buffalo, site of the previous year's 31–0 defeat. The Patriots gave up a 98-yard kick return to Terrence McGee late in the first quarter, and a 41-yard touchdown pass from Drew Bledsoe to Eric Moulds gave the Bills a 17–10 lead with 2:43 to go in the first half. The Patriots responded quickly with a 30-yard touchdown from Brady to David Patten. So, it was tied 17–17 at halftime, and stayed that way into the fourth quarter.

The Patriots took the lead with 11 minutes to play when Brady threw a 2-yard touchdown pass to Graham. The Bills drove the ball to the Patriots' 17-yard line and looked to be on the verge of tying the game, but on fourth-and-3, and with under three minutes to go in the game, the **Bills called a naked bootleg for the slow-footed Bledsoe. It didn't work!** Tedy Bruschi raced into the backfield untouched and knocked the ball out of Bledsoe's hands. Richard Seymour picked up the loose ball and ran 68 yards for the game-clinching touchdown. The 31–17 win was the Patriots' 18th in a row, tying a record held by four other NFL teams: the Chicago Bears in 1933–34 and in 1941–42; the Miami Dolphins in 1972–73; San Francisco in 1989–90; and Denver in 1997–98.

The Patriots broke the record the following week at home against the Dolphins. Brady completed only seven passes for 76 yards, the worst statistical output of his career, but he also had two touchdown passes, and the Patriots cruised to an easy 24–10 victory. **Safety Rodney Harrison and defensive end Richard Seymour dumped a bucket of ice water on Belichick when the game ended.**

"I did tell the team that no other team in pro football has done what they did," Belichick said. "We're going to try to get a little more than that. We didn't dwell on it or think about it. We didn't spend a lot of time and energy on it."

> New England Patriots head coach Bill Belichick congratulates quarterback Tom Brady after the Patriots won their 19th game in a row, a 24-10 win over the Miami Dolphins at Gillette Stadium in Foxborough, Mass. Sunday, Oct. 10, 2004. AP PHOTO/WINSLOW TOWNSON

Quick Feet

The game also featured future Patriots wide receiver Wes Welker filling in as the Dolphins placekicker. Welker, who played soccer as a kid and had his only extra point attempt in college blocked, was pressed into service when Olindo Mare injured his right calf during pregame warmups. Welker was a rookie punt returner playing in his fifth NFL game, but went 2-for-2 on his first kicks as a pro. Swinging left-footed he made an extra point and a 29-yard field goal. His kicks were merely footnotes, however, in the Patriots' record-setting performance.

With the Patriots' 20th straight win the following week at home against the Seattle Seahawks, they also tied the record of 17 consecutive regular-season wins. The Patriots jumped out to a 10–0 lead by intercepting former Boston College quarterback Matt Hasselbeck twice. McGinest had one of the picks, and Corey Dillon rushed in from the 1-yard line five plays later. Ty Law had the other interception, the 36th of his career, tying him with Raymond Clayborn for the Patriots' franchise record.

Following a Tom Brady 6-yard touchdown pass to David Patten, the Patriots were cruising, and held a 17–0 lead, but the Seahawks would not go down easily. On the first play of the fourth quarter, Seattle's Michael Boulware strip sacked Brady and ripped his helmet off in the process. The Seahawks recovered the fumble, but failed to score. The next time the Patriots had the ball, Boulware picked off a pass by Brady, and this time Seattle was able to convert the turnover into points. Shaun Alexander rushed in from 9 yards out, and then Hasselbeck connected with Jerramy Stevens for the two-point conversion. Suddenly, the Patriots' lead was just 20–17 with 11 minutes to go in the game.

The teams traded field goals, and later, facing a third-and-7 with 2:45 to go, Brady threw deep down the left side to his speediest wide receiver, Bethel Johnson, who had been inactive the week before because he wasn't quite getting the Patriots' complicated playbook. But all he had to do on this play was sprint as fast as he could!

Johnson dove for the ball and wrapped his arms under it as he landed hard on the ground. He had the wind knocked out of him, but he held on to the ball. The catch was challenged by the Seahawks, but the replays showed Johnson making a sensational catch. It was a 48-yard reception, and two plays later, Dillon iced the game with a 9-yard touchdown run. The Patriots won again, 30–20!

The streak continued with another hard-fought battle against the undefeated New York Jets. Both teams entered the game with 5-0 records, but of course, the Patriots were looking to extend their winning streak to 21 games. The Jets were the first to find the end zone with 1:55 to go in the first half. Chad Pennington ran a 1-yard bootleg to put the Jets up, 7–6. Brady answered by running the two-minute offense to perfection. With five seconds to go before the half, he hit David Patten with a 7-yard touchdown pass to put the Patriots up, 13–7. And that would be the final score.

Neither team could muster any offense in the second half, but on the Jets' final drive of the game, they moved the ball from their own 14 to the Patriots 30. The Patriot defense needed to come up with another stand, and it did. On fourth-and-8, Pennington's pass was knocked away by Rodney Harrison, and the Jets were just like the previous 20 teams the Patriots had faced. They were losers!

Four days after the Boston Red Sox won their first World Series in 86 years, the Patriots felt once again what it was like to lose a game. The Patriots lost for the first time in 398 days when they went to Pittsburgh and fell to the Steelers and their rookie quarterback Ben Roethlisberger, 34–20. Roethlisberger had replaced Tommy Maddox, and was undefeated in five games as a starter.

"They outcoached us. They outplayed us," Belichick said for the first time since a September 28, 2003, loss to the Redskins. "We did not do much right. We got beat. We got killed. When we turn the ball over and can't stop them on top of that, we're dead."

The Patriots were without Corey Dillon, who sat out with a bruised thigh, and then they lost Ty Law to a foot injury in the first quarter. On the very next play after Law limped off the field, Roethlisberger beat Law's replacement, Randall Gay, with a 47-yard touchdown pass to Plaxico Burress. That was the first of three Pittsburgh touchdowns in three minutes and 33 seconds!

On the Patriots' first play from scrimmage after the kickoff, Brady was sacked by linebacker Joe Porter and fumbled the ball away. The Steelers recovered and five plays later,

Roethlisberger threw another touchdown pass to Burress. Again, on the first play from scrimmage following the kickoff, Brady turned the ball over. **This → time his pass was picked off by Deshea Townsend, who ran it back for a touchdown.** Still in the first quarter, the Patriots were down 21–3. A short touchdown pass from Brady to David Givens would make it 24–10 before the half, but any real chance of making a comeback ended on the Patriots' first play of the third quarter. Kevin Faulk fumbled the ball, and the Steelers recovered. Jerome Bettis took the ball over the goal line four plays later to make it a 31–10 Steelers lead.

The Patriots finished with four turnovers, and were outrushed 221–5. Their winning streak snapped at 21 games, but their home winning streak would extend into the 2005 season, and would also last an NFL record 21 games.

> Pittsburgh Steelers cornerback Deshea Townsend (26) returns a first quarter intercepted pass by New England Patriots quarterback Tom Brady for a touchdown in NFL action Sunday, Oct. 31, 2004, in Pittsburgh.
AP PHOTO/GENE J. PUSKAR

The Patriots began a more modest winning streak of six games the following week in St. Louis in what Bill Belichick characterized as "probably as complete a victory as I've ever been around." The Patriots' recipe for success included wide receiver Troy Brown being used on defense as a cornerback, linebacker Mike Vrabel being used on offense to catch a touchdown pass, and **placekicker Adam Vinatieri throwing a touchdown pass on a fake field goal.** The Patriots' defense also sacked Rams quarterback Marc Bulger five times, forced him to fumble once, and picked off one of his passes. And Corey Dillon returned to rush for 112 yards, including a 5-yard touchdown. The Patriots won easily, 40–22.

> Wide receiver Troy Brown #80 of the New England Patriots celebrates a touchdown against the St. Louis Rams at the Edward Jones Dome on Nov. 7, 2004, in St. Louis, Missouri. The Patriots defeated the Rams 40–22.
AP PHOTO/SCOTT BOEHM

It was truly a remarkable team effort! Starting cornerbacks Tyrone Poole and Ty Law were both out with injuries, so when Asante Samuel was knocked out of the game with a bad shoulder on the Rams' second play, the Patriots were forced to use Earthwind Moreland, who had been activated from the practice squad earlier in the week, and wide receiver Troy Brown, as emergency cornerbacks. Brown finished the game with three catches and three tackles.

"It doesn't take much to play defensive back when all you do is grab a hold of a guy," Rams head coach Mike Martz complained. "I wouldn't get too excited about him as a DB."

Brown also contributed on special teams when he caught Vinatieri's touchdown pass, and the next week, Brown grabbed his first career interception. The Patriots were home against the Buffalo Bills, and Brown, who had 12 touchdown passes thrown to him by Drew Bledsoe when both were Patriots, intercepted Bledsoe, helping the Patriots win again, 29–6. Vinatieri kicked five field goals in the game and became the second Patriots player to score 1,000 points. Gino Cappelletti still held the franchise record with 1,130 points.

On Monday night, November 22, 2004, the Patriots played again without cornerbacks Poole, Law, and Samuel, and they were torched by the Kansas City Chiefs for 381 yards passing. But the Patriots won the game, 27–19. The following Sunday, the Patriots won their fourth in a row in a rain-soaked defensive battle with the Baltimore Ravens. The turning point of the game came 45 seconds after Dillon ran in a 1-yard touchdown and a two-point conversion to give the Patriots a

> Baltimore Ravens quarterback Kyle Boller (7) fumbles as he is hit by New England Patriots linebacker Teddy Bruschi (54) during fourth quarter action of their AFC contest in Foxborough, Mass., Sunday afternoon Nov. 28, 2004. The ball was recovered by the Patriots in the Ravens end zone resulting in a Patriots touchdown. AP PHOTO/WINSLOW TOWNSON

17–3 lead in the fourth quarter. When the Ravens got the ball back, their quarterback Kyle Boller was sacked on consecutive plays by Ted Johnson and Tedy Bruschi. **On the second sack, the soggy ball squirted free, and backup defensive end Jarvis Green recovered the ball in the end zone.** The Patriots, who set an NFL record by scoring first in a 16th straight regular-season game, went on to win, 24–3.

Their next game was much easier. Bethel Johnson returned the opening kickoff 93 yards, and the Patriots never looked back, beating the Cleveland Browns, 42–15. The Patriots also got **a defensive touchdown on a 41-yard fumble return by Randall Gay,** and four offensive touchdowns, including two from Dillon.

> New England Patriots cornerback Randall Gay returns a fumble for a 41-yard touchdown against the Baltimore Ravens Sunday, Dec. 5, 2004. After Gay picked up the fumble he felt someone pulling on his jersey. It was Patriots linebacker Willie McGinest, trying to slow his teammate down so he can set up a block. That's the way things were going for New England those days: No one could stop them except for themselves. AP PHOTO/WINSLOW TOWNSON

The Patriots clinched a playoff berth at home in Week 14 against the Cincinnati Bengals. The victory was especially satisfying for Dillon, who never made the playoffs in seven seasons with the Bengals. He ran for 88 yards and a touchdown against his former team.

"I approached it like I approached every other game," Dillon said. "I'm pretty sure every-body's sitting here waiting for me to say something wild and negative about Cincinnati. It's not going to happen. I respect those guys."

Tom Brady threw a 48-yard touchdown pass to David Patten in the first half to give the Patriots a 14–7 lead. It was the longest touchdown play of the season for the Patriots. Twelve seconds later, **Asante Samuel**  **intercepted Carson Palmer and ran the ball back 34 yards for the touchdown.** The Patriots scored again before the half on a 4-yard pass to Kevin Faulk, and took a 28–14 lead. The Bengals were still two touchdowns down in the fourth quarter when backup quarterback Jon Kitna was intercepted by Troy Brown in the end zone. It proved to be a huge play in the game as the Patriots held on to win, 35–28. It was also Brown's third interception of the season, tying him with Eugene Wilson for the team lead.

The Patriots played the game against Cincinnati knowing their offensive coordinator, Charlie Weis, would be leaving at the end of the season to take the head coaching job at Notre Dame. News broke that day, but the players already knew Weis had accepted the position. After the game,

> New England Patriots cornerback Asante Samuel (22) is congratulated by teammate Rodney Harrison after Asante intercepted a second quarter pass and returned it 34 yards for a touchdown in the Patriots' 35–28 win at Gillette Stadium in Foxborough, Mass. Sunday, Dec. 12, 2004.
AP PHOTO/WINSLOW TOWNSON

Weis flew to South Bend, Indiana, to meet with his team. He told them he'd be staying with the Patriots through the playoffs. Back in Foxborough, Brady told CBS: **"Even though he's leaving, I think everyone's going to enjoy these last few games, and hopefully we send him out the right way."**

But the Patriots, a team that looks to avoid distractions at all costs, traveled to Miami to face a 2-11 Dolphins team—and lost in a shocking upset. With a playoff berth secured, but still fighting for home-field advantage in the playoffs, the Patriots blew an 11-point lead with under four minutes to play against a team whose head coach had resigned six weeks earlier.

> In this Feb. 6, 2005, photo, New England Patriots offensive coordinator Charlie Weis, left, head coach Bill Belichick, and defensive coordinator Romeo Crennel, right, celebrate after the Patriots beat the Philadelphia Eagles, 24–21 in Super Bowl XXXIX in Jacksonville, Fla. Notre Dame fired coach Charlie Weis on Monday, Nov. 30, 2009, after a string of disappointing seasons that was capped by an agonizing four-game losing streak. Athletic director Jack Swarbrick announced the decision, saying in a news release: "We have great expectations for our football program, and we have not been able to meet those expectations." AP PHOTO/DAVID J. PHILLIP

The Patriots took a 21–17 lead on a 2-yard touchdown pass from Brady to Dillon late in the third quarter, and then extended the lead with 3:59 to play when Brady threw his third touchdown pass of the game to Daniel Graham. The Dolphins marched down the field and scored on a 1-yard run by Sammy Morris. They failed on the two-point conversion attempt and trailed 28–23, but when the Patriots got the ball back, Brady made an uncharacteristic mistake. While he was being sacked by Jason Taylor, he threw the ball right to Brendon Ayanbadejo, giving Miami the ball at the Patriots' 21-yard line with 1:45 to play. The Patriots' defense forced two incompletions, but on fourth-and-10, A. J. Feeley threw a 21-yard game-winning touchdown to Derrius Thompson, who beat Troy Brown to the ball. The Dolphins won 29–28, stunning the Patriots and handing them just their second loss in 29 games.

The Patriots rebounded with a dominating defensive performance at the Meadowlands against the Jets, and Brady rebounded from tying his career high with four interceptions against Miami by throwing a couple of touchdown passes in a 23–7 win. The Patriots kept the Jets off the scoreboard until midway into the fourth quarter, and they held Curtis Martin, who entered

> New England Patriots running back Corey Dillon breaks through a hole in the line and escapes the grasp of New York Jets' Jonathan Vilma, bottom and Terrell Buckley, left, during the third quarter Sunday, Dec. 26, 2004, in East Rutherford, N.J. Dillon rushed for 89 yards and the Patriots won 23–7. AP PHOTO/JULIE JACOBSON

the game as the NFL's leading rusher, to just 33 yards on 13 carries. Meanwhile, **Dillon ran for 89 yards** and broke Martin's Patriots franchise record for rushing yards in a season. Dillon would finish the year with a career-best 1,635 yards. The victory over the Jets also secured a first-round bye in the playoffs for the Patriots, but they learned the road to the Super Bowl would go through Pittsburgh when the Steelers earned the top seed with a win over Baltimore.

Without much to play for, the Patriots closed out the regular season with a 21–7 win over San Francisco, dropping the 49ers record to 2-14 while the Patriots finished 14-2. The Patriots' streak of scoring first in 23 consecutive games came to an end, and the Patriots ended up scoring 437 points, four fewer than the team record set in 1980.

The Patriots had played the final five games of the regular season without three-time Pro Bowl defensive end Richard Seymour, who was out with a knee injury. Then, prior to the Miami game, the Patriots placed cornerback Tyrone Poole on the Injured Reserve list, ending his season. And just as the playoffs were set to begin, the Patriots announced Ty Law would also be put on the Injured Reserve list. Law had broken a bone in the top of his foot in the Steelers game, and didn't play again in 2004. So, with a rash of injuries to their defense, the Patriots hosted the fifth-highest-scoring team in NFL history, Peyton Manning's Indianapolis Colts. And once again, the Patriots made one of the best quarterbacks of all time look bad. Perhaps, the Patriots were supremely motivated by Mike Vanderjagt's pregame comments. After the Colts had dominated Denver 49–24 in the first round of the playoffs, Vanderjagt told reporters he didn't think the Patriots were as good as they were in the beginning of the year, and that "they're ripe for the picking."

Patriot safety Rodney Harrison countered by calling Vanderjagt "Vanderjerk," and then Harrison went out and forced a fumble and intercepted Manning's last pass of the game in the end zone. The Patriots weren't ripe for the picking after all. They ended the Colts' season right where it began—in Foxborough. And they held the Colts to nearly 30 points below their season average, keeping an offense that had scored 61 touchdowns during the regular season out of the end zone.

The Patriots were successful in keeping the ball out of Manning's hands, controlling the clock for nearly 38 minutes. Corey Dillon ran for 144 yards in his playoff debut, and the Patriots had 210 yards rushing as a team. Brady threw a 5-yard touchdown pass to David Givens in the third quarter, and finished a 94-yard drive with his own 1-yard touchdown run, and the Patriots rolled to a 20–3 win.

"It was just the best game plan that we've had since I've been here," Harrison said.

Manning fell to 0-7 in Foxborough while Brady improved to 7-0 in the postseason.

> New England Patriots quarterback Tom Brady, left, and Indianapolis Colts quarterback Peyton Manning shake hands after their AFC divisional playoff game at Gillette Stadium, in this Jan. 16, 2005, file photo, in Foxborough, Mass. The Patriots won, 20–3. The two teams meet Sunday night, Nov. 5, 2006, in Foxborough. Manning is 86-57 as a starting quarterback during a career that is getting more distinguished every week. But he is just 1-7 in Foxborough. AP PHOTO/ CHARLES KRUPA

To get back to the Super Bowl, the Patriots would have to beat the Steelers in Pittsburgh, something they had done to get to the Super Bowl three years earlier, but something they had failed to do three months earlier when their winning streak was snapped. The Steelers earned home-field advantage by going 15-1, and they were 13-0 with rookie Ben Roethlisberger at quarterback. They advanced to the AFC championship with an overtime victory against the Jets, who had two chances to kick a game-winning field goal in regulation, but Doug Brien missed them both.

The Patriots and Steelers met at Heinz Field on January 23, 2005. The gametime temperature was 11 degrees with a wind chill of minus 1 at kickoff. Roethlisberger, whose personal winning streak was 27 games going back to his final season at Miami of Ohio, had his first pass of the game intercepted by Eugene Wilson. That led to a 48-yard field goal by Vinatieri. Pittsburgh got

> New England Patriots' Rodney Harrison returns an interception 87 yards for a touchdown in the second quarter of the AFC Championship game against the Pittsburgh Steelers Sunday, Jan. 23, 2005, in Pittsburgh. AP PHOTO/STEPHAN SAVOIA

the ball back and drove to the Patriots' 39-yard line where, on fourth-and-1, Jerome Bettis ran the ball into a wall of Patriots. Roosevelt Colvin stripped the ball away and Mike Vrabel recovered it for the Patriots. On the very next play, Brady hit Deion Branch on a 60-yard post pattern for a touchdown, and a 10–0 lead. Brady also hit Branch for 45 yards to set up a 9-yard touchdown throw to David Givens that gave the Patriots a 17–3 lead. The Steelers, who had allowed the fewest points in the league during the regular season, were on their way to giving up 41 points!

The Steelers' third turnover came with just over two minutes left in the first half, but effectively ended the game. Roethlisberger threw in the direction of tight end Jerame Tuman, but **Rodney Harrison jumped the route, picked off the pass, and ran it back 87 yards for a touchdown!** The Patriots led 24–3.

Steelers fans didn't boo then, but they booed head coach Bill Cowher's early fourth quarter decision to kick a field goal instead of going for a touchdown on fourth-and-goal from the 2. The field goal made the score 31–20 with 13 1/2 minutes to play, but after another Vinatieri field goal and another Eugene Wilson interception, the Patriots cruised to a 41–27 victory, and their third trip to the Super Bowl in four years. Tom Brady was 14-of-21 for 207 yards and no interceptions and improved to 8-0 in the playoffs, and Bill Belichick tied Vince Lombardi with the best postseason record at 9-1.

"It's very flattering to be mentioned in the same breath with Vince Lombardi," Belichick said. "That's why the trophy has his name on it."

The Patriots, now 14-0 since 2001 in rematches with the same starting quarterback, faced the Philadelphia Eagles in Super Bowl XXXIX on February 6 at Alltel Stadium in Jacksonville, Florida. The first quarter was a defensive battle. Philadelphia forced the Patriots to punt on each of their first four possessions, and the Patriots' defense was able to keep the game scoreless when Rodney Harrison intercepted a Donovan McNabb pass at the New England 4-yard line. On the Eagles' first possession of the second quarter, they put together an 81-yard drive culminating in a 6-yard touchdown strike from McNabb to L. J. Smith.

The Patriots responded with an impressive drive, moving the ball 80 yards on six plays, including a 25-yard run by Corey Dillon to the Eagles' 7-yard line, but two plays later the Patriots committed their first turnover of the postseason when Brady fumbled the ball away. His hand hit Kevin Faulk's hip, and the Eagles' Darwin Walker recovered the ball at the Eagles' 13. The Patriots' defense forced a quick three-and-out, and after a 29-yard Eagle punt, the Patriots only needed to go 37 yards to tie the game. A 4-yard touchdown pass to David Givens with 1:16 on

the clock put the Patriots on the board. The game was tied 7–7 at halftime, and after Mike Vrabel and Brian Westbrook caught touchdown passes in the third quarter, it was tied 14–14 after three quarters.

The Patriots finally took control of the game when Dillon scored from 2 yards out early in the fourth quarter, and Adam Vinatieri followed with a field goal five minutes later to make it 24–14. There was still 8:40 to play, so the Eagles had time to make it interesting. And they did! McNabb hit Greg Lewis for a 30-yard touchdown to make it 24–21 with 1:48 to go, and the Eagles' defense forced the Patriots to punt, giving the Eagles the ball back with 46 seconds left. Their final drive began on

> Super Bowl XXXIX Most Valuable Player Deion Branch of the New England Patriots holds up the Vince Lombardi trophy after the Patriots beat the Philadelphia Eagles, 24–21 in Jacksonville, Fla., Sunday, Feb. 6, 2005. AP PHOTO/CHRIS O'MEARA

Coaching Victories

Bill Belichick has the most playoff victories among NFL coaches with a record of 26-10.

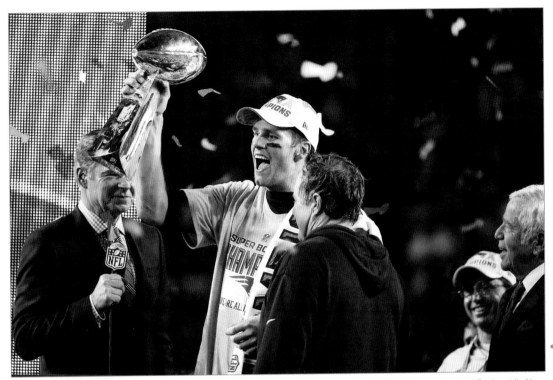

> Sportscaster Dan Patrick holds the microphone as New England Patriots quarterback Tom Brady (12) holds up the Lombardi Trophy while New England Patriots head coach Bill Belichick and Patriots owner Robert Kraft watch while confetti flies in celebration after the NFL Super Bowl XLIX football game against the Seattle Seahawks on Sunday, Feb. 1, 2015, in Glendale, Ariz. The Patriots won the game 28–24.
AP PHOTO/PAUL SPINELLI

their own 4, and ended three plays later when Rodney Harrison picked off his second pass of the game. The Patriots were the eighth team to win back-to-back Super Bowls. **Wide receiver Deion Branch drove away with the Super Bowl MVP award,** catching 11 passes for 133 yards, and Brady, whose 94-year-old grandmother had passed away four days earlier, finished with 236 yards and two touchdowns.

It was already known that offensive coordinator Charlie Weis was on his way to Notre Dame, and shortly after the game ended, 57-year-old defensive coordinator Romeo Crennel accepted a job as the head coach of the Cleveland Browns. So, while the king (Belichick) was losing two key members of his court, **there was no doubt that with their third Super Bowl victory in four years, the Patriots were a football dynasty!**

CHAPTER FIVE

THE
2007 BOSTON RED SOX

Principal Owner:
John Henry

General Manager:
Theo Epstein

Manager:
Terry Francona

Regular Season Record:
96-66

Regular Season Finish:
AL East Champions

Playoff Results:
Wild Card Round—Boston Red Sox defeated
Los Angeles Angels (3–0)

Divisional Round—Boston Red Sox defeated
Cleveland Indians (4–3)

World Series:
Boston Red Sox defeated
Colorado Rockies (4–0)

Awards:
World Series MVP: 3B Mike Lowell

All-Stars: OF Manny Ramirez, DH David Ortiz,
3B Mike Lowell, P Josh Beckett,
RP Jonathan Papelbon

After winning their first World Series in 86 years, the Red Sox became a team in decline. In 2005, they won 95 games and were swept out of the first round of the playoffs by the Chicago White Sox, who went on to win the World Series ending their own 88-year drought. In 2006, the Red Sox dropped to 86 wins, good for third place in the American League East, and failed to make the playoffs. It was time to reverse the downward trend. So, the Red Sox dove into the free-agent waters and landed three big fish: Japanese pitcher Daisuke Matsuzaka, outfielder J. D. Drew, and shortstop Julio Lugo.

Matsuzaka had been selected to six All-Star teams in seven seasons while pitching for the Seibu Lions in the Nippon Professional League, and the Red Sox would have to win the rights to negotiate with him by paying a posting fee to the Lions. The Red Sox far outbid the Yankees, Mets, and Rangers by offering the Lions the unique and specific sum of $51,111,111.11. Majority owner John Henry chose the amount, because he had been referred to as Investor 11 when he was secretly bidding on the Red Sox in 2001. Henry wanted as many 11s in the bid as possible. After winning the bidding rights on November 14, the

Red Sox had 30 days to negotiate a deal with Matsuzaka. On the 29th day of negotiations, they signed Matsuzaka to a six-year, $52 million contract.

While they were negotiating with Matsuzaka, the Red Sox signed another Japanese pitcher, left-handed reliever Hideki Okajima, to a two-year, $2.5 million contract. Okajima was a free agent who didn't require a posting fee to sign, and the Red Sox envisioned him as a setup man to second-year closer Jonathan Papelbon. In 2006, Papelbon had 35 saves and a 0.92 ERA, and finished second in Rookie of the Year voting, but the Red Sox would experiment with him as a starter in spring training. Less than two weeks before the start of the season, the Red Sox decided to move Papelbon back to his role as the closer.

Also during the Matsuzaka negotiations, the Red Sox committed $106 million to Drew and Lugo. Drew was a 31-year-old center fielder whom the Red Sox would put in right field to replace free agent Trot Nixon. Drew had just driven in 100 runs for the Dodgers, and the Red Sox gave him a five-year, $70 million contract. Lugo, also 31, signed a four-year, $36 million deal, and he would replace free agent shortstop Alex González. Meanwhile, the Red Sox further improved their defense and their lineup by awarding the second-base job to rookie Dustin Pedroia. The Red Sox now had a team that would win its first American League East title in 12 years, and win more games than any team in baseball (96), and of course, win New England's fifth championship in six years!

The Red Sox opened the season at Kaufman Stadium in Kansas City. Kevin Youkilis scored the season's first run on a double by David Ortiz, and the Royals scored the next seven runs. Curt Schilling lasted only four innings and gave up five runs as the Red Sox lost the opener, 7–1. Two days later in temperatures 30 degrees colder, the Red Sox won by the exact

MVP Stats

In 2008, Dustin Pedroia became the 10th Red Sox player to win the American League MVP Award. Ted Williams won it twice.

> Boston Red Sox pitcher Josh Beckett throws during the first inning in a baseball game with the Kansas City Royals, Wednesday, April 4, 2007, in Kansas City, Mo. AP PHOTO/DICK WHIPPLE

same score. Youkilis hit the team's first home run of the year, and Josh Beckett picked up the first of the 20 wins he'd earn that year. Beckett was acquired along with third baseman Mike Lowell prior to the 2006 season in a trade with the Florida Marlins. The Red Sox sent four prospects to Florida, including highly regarded shortstop Hanley Ramírez. The deal didn't look good when Beckett posted a 5.01 ERA and surrendered 36 home runs in his first year with the Red Sox while Ramírez went on to win the National League Rookie of the Year Award, but **Beckett finished second in the Cy Young voting in 2007,** and both he and Lowell were All-Stars that year as well.

Matsuzaka's debut was also at Kaufman Stadium. He began his big-league career by striking out 10 Kansas City Royals in seven innings and picking up a 4–1 win. The gametime temperature was 36 degrees, and Matsuzaka dealt with it by stepping off the mound to do jumping jacks and click his heels together. The crowd booed!

The Red Sox went 3-3 on their road trip to start the season, and returned to Fenway Park to pound the Seattle Mariners 14–3 in their home opener. **J. D. Drew introduced himself to the Fenway Faithful by hitting his first home run of the year**, and Beckett was outstanding once again, striking out eight and allowing just two hits in seven innings. The next day, the Red Sox were one-hit by Seattle's 21-year-old sensation Félix Hernández. Drew broke up the no-hitter with a solid single on the first pitch of the eighth inning. Matsuzaka pitched well again, but took the loss. The Red Sox were just 4-4 and batting .238 as a team, but they swept the Angels, outscoring them 25–3, and went on to win 29 of their next 40 games. The Red Sox took over first place in the East on April 18 and never relinquished it.

> Seattle Mariners starter Jeff Weaver looks toward the outfield as Boston Red Sox' J. D. Drew (7) crosses home plate on his two-run homer during the second inning of their baseball game in Boston, Tuesday, April 10, 2007. Weaver gave up seven runs on seven hits in his two-inning outing. AP PHOTO/CHARLES KRUPA

After winning two out of three in Toronto, the Red Sox came home on April 20 and proceeded to sweep the Yankees in three close games. They won the series opener when they rallied for five runs in the eighth inning to erase a 6–2 deficit. Once again, the Red Sox were able to beat Mariano Rivera. Jason Varitek singled home a run off him. Coco Crisp followed with a two-run triple that tied the game, and Alex Cora brought home the game-winning run with a bloop single over a drawn-in infield. With Papelbon unavailable, Okajima picked up his first big-league save as the Red Sox won, 7–6.

Josh Beckett improved to 4-0 when the Red Sox took the second game of the series, 7–5, and then the Red Sox made history in the series finale. Manny Ramírez, Drew, Lowell, and Varitek

> Boston Red Sox' Jason Varitek hits the fourth consecutive home run of the third inning against New York Yankees pitcher Chase Wright during their baseball game at Fenway Park in Boston Sunday, April 22, 2007. AP PHOTO/ELISE AMENDOLA

> Boston Red Sox' Mike Lowell, right, is congratulated by teammate Jason Varitek after his three-run home run off New York Yankees pitcher Scott Proctor in the seventh inning of their baseball game at Fenway Park in Boston Sunday, April 22, 2007, in Boston. At center is New York Yankees catcher Wil Nieves. AP PHOTO/ELISE AMENDOLA

hit consecutive home runs in the third inning **making the Red Sox just the fifth team in major-league history to hit four consecutive homers.** Each one came off Yankees rookie Chase Wright.

The Red Sox closed April by winning two of three against the Yankees in New York, finishing the month 16-8. They were in first place, and the Yankees, who had won nine straight AL East titles, were in last. Beckett was 5-0. David Ortiz, who set a team record with 54 home runs in 2006, had seven homers. And Papelbon had eight saves and had yet to give up a run. That streak ended on May 1 when he gave up a game-tying two-run homer in the ninth inning to the Oakland A's Travis Buck. The Red Sox went on to lose, 5–4, in 10 innings.

The Red Sox responded by winning 20 of the remaining 27 games in May. By month's end, the Red Sox had the best record in baseball at 36-16, and they held a 10.5-game lead over the second-place Orioles in the AL East. Along the way, Josh Beckett became the first Red Sox pitcher to win his first seven starts of a season since Rogelio "Roger" Moret won eight straight in 1973 to tie a franchise record held by Babe Ruth and Dave Ferriss. Beckett failed to win an eighth consecutive start when he was forced to leave a game against the Orioles with a torn flap of skin on his right middle finger. Beckett would go on the 15-day disabled list, but that game is better remembered as the one in which the Red Sox scored six runs in the bottom of the ninth inning to win, 6–5. The unexpected Mother's Day gift began when Orioles catcher Ramon Hernandez dropped a one-out popup in the infield for an error that allowed Coco Crisp to reach base safely. Orioles manager Sam Perlozzo decided to lift starting pitcher Jeremy Guthrie, who was working on a three-hit shutout. Perlozzo would regret that decision. The Red Sox followed with four hits and two walks. Jason Varitek's two-run double cut the deficit to 5–4, and with the bases loaded and two outs, Julio Lugo hit a high chopper to the right side of the infield. Millar came way off the bag to field it, and his throw to first base was dropped by reliever Chris Ray. **The tying and winning runs scored and the Red Sox had their first walkoff victory of the season.** It was a Mother's Day Miracle!

June began with a three-game series at Fenway against the last-place Yankees. The Red Sox split the first two games, but lost the series when Alex Rodriguez homered off Jonathan Papelbon in the ninth inning of the finale to lift the Yankees to a 6–5 win. The Red Sox then went to Oakland, where they lost the first three games of a four-game series. Suddenly the Red Sox, who still had the best record in baseball, also had a four-game losing streak and had dropped five of their last six games. Schilling stopped the skid by nearly throwing a no-hitter in the series finale. Oakland's Shannon Stewart singled sharply to right field with two outs in the ninth inning. Stewart swung at

➤ Boston Red Sox' Julio Lugo, center, is mobbed by teammates Wily Mo Pena, left, and J. C. Romero (32) after Lugo's hit scored the winning run in the ninth inning of Boston's 6–5 win over the Baltimore Orioles in a baseball game at Fenway Park in Boston, Sunday, May 13, 2007. The Red Sox scored six runs in the ninth inning to win. Lugo reached base on an error on the play. AP PHOTO/WINSLOW TOWNSON

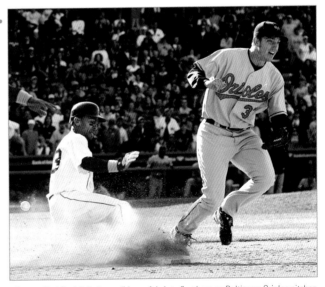

➤ Boston Red Sox' Julio Lugo slides safely into first base as Baltimore Orioles pitcher Chris Ray drops the ball, allowing the winning run to score in the ninth inning of Boston's 6–5 win over the Baltimore Orioles in a baseball game at Fenway Park in Boston Sunday, May 13, 2007. The Red Sox scored six runs in the ninth inning to win. Ray was given an error on the play. AP PHOTO/WINSLOW TOWNSON

What if...

"We get two outs, and I was sure, and I had a plan, and I shook Tek off," Schilling said. "And I get a big 'What if' for the rest of my life."

the first pitch he saw, which was a fastball that Schilling wanted to throw, and not the slider that Jason Varitek had originally called for.

Schilling retired the next batter, Mark Ellis, on a foul popup for his third career one-hitter. The Red Sox won 1–0 with David Ortiz's solo home run in the first inning accounting for the only run of the game. Nine days later, the Red Sox would win another 1–0 game, this one at home against the San Francisco Giants. Manny Ramírez homered for the game's only run, and Matsuzaka pitched seven shutout innings to improve to 8-5.

Meanwhile, Schilling's next two starts were terrible. He gave up six runs in five innings to the Rockies, and then six more runs in 4⅓ innings against the Braves. In the start against the Braves, he failed to strike anyone out for the first time in 14 years.

"It's embarrassing," Schilling said. "I never gave us a chance. You want to walk around the room and apologize to everybody. There's no excuse for a game like that."

> Boston Red Sox pitcher Curt Schilling, right, is hugged by manager Terry Francona, center, as first-base coach Luis Alicea (16) looks on at the end of a baseball game against the Oakland Athletics in Oakland, Calif., Thursday, June 7, 2007. Schilling threw a complete-game one-hit shutout in a 1–0 win over the Athletics. AP PHOTO/MARCIO JOSE SANCHEZ

> Boston Red Sox reliever Hideki Okajima, of Japan, delivers a pitch against Arizona Diamondbacks batter Conor Jackson in the eighth inning of a baseball game Saturday, June 9, 2007, in Phoenix. AP PHOTO/PAUL CONNORS

As it turned out, the excuse may have been shoulder tendinitis. Schilling was placed on the 15-day disabled list on June 19 and didn't pitch again until August 6.

The Red Sox ended up going 13-14 in June, closing out the month by losing four of five games, and then stumbling into the All-Star break on a three-game losing streak. Still, they had the best record in baseball and led the now second-place Yankees by 9.5 games. The Red Sox would send a major-league best six players to the All-Star Game in San Francisco, including Ortiz, who had 14 homers and 52 RBIs at the break, Mike Lowell who led the Red Sox with 63 RBIs, and Manny Ramírez with 45 RBIs. **Having given up only four runs in 43 innings for a 0.83 ERA in the first half, Hideki Okajima was chosen for the All-Star team,** along with Papelbon, who had 20 saves and a 1.93 ERA, and Beckett who was 12-2. Beckett didn't start the All-Star Game, but he got the win, which meant the American League team would have home-field advantage in the World Series.

The Red Sox began the second half of the season by losing five of their first eight games. Among the victories was rookie Kason Gabbard's complete-game shutout of the Kansas City Royals on July 16 at Fenway Park. **A week later another young pitcher would grab the attention of Red Sox Nation.** Twenty-three-year-old lefty Jon Lester, whose rookie season was cut short when he was diagnosed with anaplastic large cell lymphoma, made a victorious return on July 23 at Jacobs Field in Cleveland. Pitching in the big leagues for the first time in 11 months, Lester struck out six Indians in six innings and picked up the 6–2 win. It was Boston's 60th win of the year. They were 21 games over .500 and in the midst of a five-game winning streak.

In Lester's second start, he left the game in Tampa in the seventh inning with a 5–4 lead over the Rays, but Lester was denied the victory when Papelbon gave up a game-tying home run to Jonny Gomes in the ninth. The Red Sox went on to score six runs in the 12th inning to beat the Rays 12–6 for their seventh win in eight games, and they'd finish July with a seven-game lead over the Yankees and a 64-42 record. They also made a move to upgrade their bullpen at the trade deadline. On July 31, they traded Gabbard and two minor-league outfielders, David Murphy and Engel Beltré, to the Texas Rangers for the 2003 National League Cy Young Award winner, Eric Gagne. A three-time All-Star, Gagne had 16 saves and a 2.16 ERA for the Rangers. He was willing to waive his no-trade clause and to become a setup man for Papelbon, and

> Fans demonstrate their support for Boston Red Sox pitcher Jon Lester during a baseball game against the Cleveland Indians Monday, July 23, 2007, in Cleveland. Lester made his first start of the season after being diagnosed with cancer in 2006. AP PHOTO/RON SCHWANE

along with Okajima, the Red Sox hoped to have the most dominating seventh-, eighth-, and ninth-inning pitchers in baseball. It didn't really work out that way. Gagne posted a 6.75 ERA in 20 appearances for the Red Sox. On the same day as the Gagne deal, the Boston Celtics made a better trade, acquiring Kevin Garnett from the Minnesota Timberwolves. The rest is history and coming up in the next chapter!

Curt Schilling returned to the Red Sox rotation during the team's nine-game road trip in early August. In his first game back, he gave up a go-ahead home run to Maicer Izturis in the seventh inning and lost a 4–2 decision to the Angels. The Red Sox lost again the next day and their lead over the Yankees, which had been 12 games as recently as July 5, was cut to just five games. The road trip ended in Baltimore, where the Red Sox lost two out of three to the Orioles. They lost the series finale when Eric Gagne gave up a game-tying home run to Miguel Tejada in the ninth inning, and then Kyle Snyder gave up a game-winning three-run homer in the 10th inning to former Red Sox slugger Kevin Millar. The Orioles walked off with a 6–3 win, and the Red Sox limped off with a 4-5 road trip and a four-game lead over the Yankees.

The Red Sox returned home and gave up just six hits and one run in two wins over Tampa Bay. In the second victory, Mike Lowell homered in the ninth to tie the game, and then **Coco Crisp singled home Jason Varitek for the walkoff 2–1 victory**. Red Sox

> Boston Red Sox players surround Coco Crisp (hidden from view) as they celebrate his RBI single in the ninth inning that drove in the winning run in their come-from-behind 2–1 victory over the Tampa Bay Devil Rays during their baseball game in Boston on Tuesday, Aug. 14, 2007. AP PHOTO/ELISE AMENDOLA

> Boston Red Sox' Kevin Youkilis reacts after the umpires conferred and reversed a call declaring him out during seventh-inning MLB baseball action against the New York Yankees Thursday, Aug. 30, 2007 at Yankee Stadium in New York. AP PHOTO/BILL KOSTROUN

players raced on to the field to celebrate! It was just the second time all year that they had won a game when trailing after eight innings. Gagne, who had allowed seven runs in four innings over seven games since coming to the Red Sox, had struck out the side in the top of the ninth and picked up the win. Three days later, the Red Sox split a doubleheader with the visiting Angels. In the first game, a gangly right-hander named Clay Buchholz made his first big-league start, and the Red Sox treated him to a six-run first inning. David Ortiz hit his 20th home run of the year off Angels ace John Lackey, and Buchholz gave up three runs in six innings for the win. In the nightcap, the Red Sox rallied for four runs in the eighth inning. Ortiz hit a game-tying double, and Manny Ramírez doubled him home to give the Red Sox a 5–4 lead, but Gagne gave up three runs in the ninth inning, and the Red Sox lost, 7–5.

After a 4-3 homestand, the Red Sox were back out on the road for 10 games. They swept a four-game series in Chicago, outscoring the White Sox 46–7 in the process, then they went to New York and lost three straight to the Yankees. Johnny Damon hit a decisive two-run homer in the series opener as Andy Pettitte outpitched Daisuke Matsuzaka for a 5–3 win. A 45-year-old Roger Clemens then took a no-hitter into the sixth inning and beat Josh Beckett, 4–3. And in the series finale, Chien-Ming Wang took a no-hitter into the seventh inning, and the Yankees went on to win 5–0. In the ninth inning, **rookie reliever Joba Chamberlain was ejected after throwing two pitches over the head of Kevin Youkilis**. Chamberlain and Yankee manager Joe Torre claimed the pitches weren't intentional, and that no message was being sent, but Terry Francona said: "If that young man is trying to get our attention, he did a very good job."

Also of note from the Yankees series was an injury to Manny Ramírez. He left the series opener in the bottom of the seventh because of muscle spasms in his lower back. He would

> Boston Red Sox' Clay Buchholz pitches with two outs in the ninth inning to the last batter of his no-hitter, Baltimore Orioles' Nick Markakis, in a baseball game at Fenway Park in Boston, Saturday, Sept. 1, 2007. The Red Sox won 10–0. AP PHOTO/WINSLOW TOWNSON

miss the next 24 games. Four days later on September 1, the Red Sox called up rookie Jacoby Ellsbury from Pawtucket. Ellsbury played sensational defense, and batted .361 with eight stolen bases in September.

Clay Buchholz was also called up from Pawtucket on September 1, and made his second big-league start that day against the Orioles at Fenway Park. Remarkably, **Buchholz tossed a no-hitter!** The closest the Orioles came to getting a hit was a groundball up the middle off the bat of Miguel Tejada, but another rookie, Dustin Pedroia, dove for the ball and made a sensational backhanded stop. He jumped up and fired the ball to first just in time to get Tejada, who made a headfirst slide.

"When he made that play I knew something was meant to happen tonight," Buchholz said. "It was an incredible moment in my life."

> Boston Red Sox' David Ortiz (34) jumps into the arms of teammates at home plate after hitting a two-run home off Tampa Bay Devil Rays' Al Reyes in the ninth inning of a baseball game at Boston's Fenway Park, Wednesday, Sept. 12, 2007. The two-run home run gave the Red Sox a come-from-behind win over the Devil Rays 5–4. AP PHOTO/GREG M. COOPER

Buchholz completed the 17th no-hitter in Red Sox history by getting a called third strike against Nick Markakis. Jason Varitek raced out to the mound and lifted Buchholz into the air as the rest of the team ran on to the field and the crowd erupted for several minutes of a standing ovation! It was the first no-hitter by a Red Sox pitcher since Derek Lowe no-hit the Rays on April 27, 2002. The score of both games was 10–0.

The Red Sox shutout the Orioles again six days later. That game was in Baltimore and there was very nearly a brawl when Orioles pitcher Daniel Cabrera reacted to balking in a run in the fourth inning by throwing the next pitch at Dustin Pedroia's head. The benches and bull-pens emptied, but only Cabrera was ejected from the game. The Red Sox took three of four in Baltimore and came home to take two of three against the Rays. In the series finale, **David Ortiz hit a walkoff two-run homer into the first row of the right field bleachers** to beat the Rays, 5–4. That gave the Red Sox a 5.5-game lead over the Yankees, and the Yankees would arrive the next day to begin a crucial three-game series.

The Red Sox took a 7–2 lead in the series opener against the Yankees, but Hideki Okajima gave up back-to-back home runs to Jason Giambi and Robinson Canó in the eighth inning. The Yankees went on to score six runs in the inning. Papelbon took the loss when he gave up consecutive hits to Derek Jeter, Bobby Abreu, and Alex Rodriguez. The Yankees went on to win, 8–7. The Red Sox won the second game, 10–1, when Josh Beckett shut the Yankees down, allowing just one run on three hits in seven innings. And in the series finale, Derek Jeter broke up a 1–1 game in the eighth inning when he blasted a three-run homer off Schilling deep over the wall in left. The Red Sox lost, 4–3.

The Red Sox then traveled to Toronto and lost three straight to the Blue Jays. In the series opener, Blue Jays slugger Frank Thomas homered three times and the Red Sox fell, 6–1. The next day, Gagne blew his fourth save since joining the Red Sox. And in the series finale, Papelbon gave up a grand slam to Russ Adams. The Red Sox lost that game, 6–1. Meanwhile, the Yankees were sweeping the Orioles, so the Red Sox lead in the East was down to 1.5 games with nine games left to play.

On September 21, Josh Beckett stopped the Red Sox four-game losing streak by beating the Tampa Bay Rays for his 20th win of the season, and the Red Sox clinched a playoff spot the next day when another win over the Rays assured them of at least a wild card spot. The Red Sox marked the occasion with a few handshakes and high fives, but they still had their eyes set on winning their first division title since 1995. That happened a week later at home and a wild celebration ensued.

With their magic number for clinching the East down to two, the Red Sox beat the Minnesota Twins, 5–2, and then stayed at the ballpark to watch the Yankees blow a three-run

Over 20 Wins

Pedro Martinez is one of nine Red Sox pitchers to win at least 20 games in a season two or more times. Martinez did it in 1999 (23) and 2002 (20).

> Boston Red Sox' Manny Ramirez watches his game-winning home run as Los Angeles Angels catcher Jeff Mathis, right, walks away in the ninth inning in Game 2 of an American League Division Series playoff Friday, Oct. 5, 2007, at Fenway Park in Boston.
AP PHOTO/MICHAEL DWYER

lead in the ninth inning at Baltimore. When the Orioles' Melvin Mora bunted in the winning run with the bases loaded in the 10th inning, the Yankees lost, and the Red Sox were division winners! The few thousand fans who had stayed at Fenway Park to watch the Yankees on the center field scoreboard cheered as the winning run crossed the plate, and cheered again when Red Sox players came out on to the field and popped bottles of champagne. Papelbon wore spandex shorts and danced some kind of a jig barefoot through the infield to the beat of "Don't Stop Believin'" blaring over the sound system.

"I pulled my hamstring jumping off the couch," Francona said after watching the Yankees game in his office with general manager Theo Epstein and team owners John Henry and Tom Werner. "It's fun to see grown men act like little kids."

The Red Sox finished the season with 96 wins. Mike Lowell led the team with 120 RBIs. David Ortiz blasted 35 home runs. And Kevin Youkilis established an American League record with 1,079 errorless chances. The Red Sox, who had held sole possession of first place since April 18, were ready for the playoffs. Bring on the Angels!

The 2007 playoffs began at Fenway Park with Josh Beckett matched up in Game 1 against the Angels' 19-game winner, John Lackey. Beckett gave up a leadoff single and then retired the next 19 Angel hitters on his way to his third postseason shutout. Youkilis and Ortiz both hit home runs and the Red Sox took the first game, 4–0.

Manny Ramírez was the hero of Game 2 when he blasted a three-run walkoff homer with two outs in the ninth inning off Anaheim closer Francisco Rodríguez. With Julio Lugo on second base, Rodríguez came in to the game and struck out Youkilis, and then intentionally walked Ortiz to get to Ramírez. His 21st postseason home run sailed over the Green Monster and the Red Sox won, 6–3.

"I haven't been right all year," Ramírez said. "When you don't feel good and you still get hits, that's how you know you're a bad man."

The Red Sox went to Anaheim and completed the series sweep with a 9–1 rout behind seven shutout innings from Curt Schilling. Ortiz and Ramírez hit back-to-back home runs in the fourth inning, and the Red Sox blew it open with a seven-run eighth inning. Up next for the Red Sox were the Cleveland Indians, who needed four games to knock out the Yankees in the other division series.

Beckett was back on the hill to start the first game of the Championship Series at Fenway Park. The Indians countered with big left-hander C. C. Sabathia, who had won 19 games and would later edge out Beckett in the Cy Young balloting. Beckett gave up a first-inning home run to Travis Hafner, ending his postseason scoreless streak at 18 innings, but he won the duel by lasting six innings and giving up just two runs. Sabathia, meanwhile, gave up eight runs on seven hits and five walks and was pulled with one out in the fifth inning. **Once again, the → hitting stars were Ortiz and Ramírez, who reached base all ten times they batted.** What they were doing was truly remarkable! Ortiz was 7-for-9 with eight walks and a

> Boston Red Sox' David Ortiz doubles off Cleveland Indians pitcher Joe Borowski in the eighth inning during Game 1 of the American League Championship baseball series Friday, Oct. 12, 2007, at Fenway Park in Boston. Indians catcher Victor Martinez and umpire Randy Marsh watch the action. AP PHOTO/STEPHAN SAVOIA

Take Nothing for Granted

"That's a great team over there," Indians Game 4 starter Paul Byrd said. "They can easily come back and win three. We're taking absolutely nothing for granted. We'll enjoy the win for now, but we want to put them away.**"**

hit-by-pitch in the four postseason games so far. Ramirez had reached base in 11 of his last 12 at-bats, and in Game 1 against the Indians, he was walked twice with the bases loaded.

"I've never seen anything like it," Mike Lowell, said. "They're unbelievable. For them to get on base like they did today is a little bit ridiculous."

Ramírez also homered in Game 2, which gave him a record 23 postseason home runs, and Ortiz reached base for a record-tying 10th consecutive at-bat, but the Red Sox lost the game when the Indians scored seven runs in the 11th inning. The game lasted five hours and 14 minutes, and the Red Sox lost, 13–6.

The Red Sox had turned to Schilling to start Game 2, moving him up in the rotation ahead of Daisuke Matsuzaka. Schilling's postseason prowess was well documented. He was 9-2 with a 1.93 ERA in 16 playoff starts, but he gave up home runs to Jhonny Peralta and Grady Sizemore and was knocked out in the fifth inning. The Red Sox temporarily took a 6–5 lead when Ramírez and Lowell hit back-to-back home runs in the fifth inning, but the Indians tied it up in the sixth on a Franklin Gutiérrez RBI groundout. In the 11th, Trot Nixon haunted his former team by singling to right-center off Javier López driving home the go-ahead run. Nixon had spent 13 years in the Red Sox organization, but left as a free agent during the offseason. He batted just .251 with three home runs during the regular season.

López gave up two more runs before Jon Lester came in and gave up an RBI double to Peralta and a three-run homer to Gutiérrez. The seven runs scored by Cleveland was a playoff record for an extra inning.

The series moved to Cleveland for Game 3, where Matsuzaka gave up a two-run homer to Kenny Lofton in the second inning and two more runs in the fifth before exiting on the wrong side of a 4–0 score. Indians starter Jake Westbrook gave up only a two-run homer to Jason Varitek in the seventh, and the Red Sox lost, 4–2.

The Red Sox fell into a 3–1 hole in the series when the Indians rode a seven-run fifth inning to victory in Game 4. Casey Blake got the rally started with a leadoff homer against Tim Wakefield, and Blake drove home the seventh run of the inning with a single off Manny Delcarmen.

Beckett got the comeback started with another dominant performance in Game 5, allowing just one run in eight innings. If the Indians were trying to distract him by having his ex-girlfriend, country singer Danielle Peck, sing the national anthem, it didn't work.

"I don't get paid to make those (expletive) decisions," Beckett said about Peck being chosen to sing on the same night he was pitching. "She's a friend of mine. That doesn't bother me at all. Thanks for flying one of my friends to the game so she could watch it for free."

Beckett outdueled Sabathia for the second time in the series. **Kevin Youkilis homered in the first inning and tripled in another run in the seventh**, and the Red Sox won easily, 7–1.

➤ Boston Red Sox' Kevin Youkilis watches his solo home run off Cleveland Indians pitcher C. C. Sabathia in the first inning of Game 5 of the American League Championship baseball series Thursday, Oct. 18, 2007, in Cleveland. Umpire Gary Cederstrom watches from behind the plate. AP PHOTO/AMY SANCETTA

> Boston Red Sox' J. D. Drew, right, gets congratulations from David Ortiz, left rear, and Kevin Youkilis (20) after hitting a grand slam off (shown below) Cleveland Indians pitcher Fausto Carmona in the first inning in Game 6 of the American League Championship baseball series Saturday, Oct. 20, 2007, at Fenway Park in Boston.
AP PHOTO/WINSLOW TOWNSON

> AP PHOTO/WINSLOW TOWNSON

Back at Fenway Park for Game 6, J. D. Drew hit a grand slam in the first inning off the Indians other 19-game winner, Fausto Carmona. Fans who had booed Drew, who had only one hit in the playoffs, cheered wildly as his line drive sailed into the camera box in center field. **Drew raised his fist as he rounded the bases, and the fans didn't stop cheering until he came back out of the dugout for a curtain call.** The Red Sox scored six more runs in the third inning. Schilling pitched a strong seven innings, and the Red Sox forced a decisive Game 7 with a 12–2 win.

With a chance to get back to the World Series, the Red Sox handed the ball to Daisuke Matsuzaka, who had struggled with an ERA of 6.75 in his first two postseason starts. Matsuzaka delivered an efficient five innings, allowing two runs before leaving with a narrow, 3–2 lead. **Dustin Pedroia led the Red Sox 14-hit attack with five RBIs, and his homer in the seventh extended the Red Sox lead to 5–2.** The Red Sox tacked on six more runs in the eighth, including another home run by Youkilis. And with the Red Sox leading 11–2, Coco Crisp raced into the center field triangle to track down the final out of the game. He crashed into the wall and fell to the ground as the Red Sox began celebrating. Varitek ran out from behind the plate and leaped into Papelbon's arms. The Red Sox were American League champions once again!

Waiting for the Red Sox were the Colorado Rockies, who were on an amazing late-season surge. They had squeaked into the playoffs by winning 12 of their last 13 regular-season games, and then won an exciting one-game playoff against the San Diego Padres when they scored three runs in the bottom of the 13th inning to win, 3–2. The Rockies then carried that momentum into the playoffs and swept away both the Phillies and the Diamondbacks. By the time the Red Sox got to them, the Rockies had won 10 in a row and 20 of their last 21 games. It appeared nothing could stop them — until Josh Beckett did just that.

Beckett continued his masterful postseason run by allowing just one run over seven innings, improving his 2007 playoff record to 4-0 with a 1.20 ERA. The Red Sox supported him with a 17-hit outburst that began with Pedroia leading off the home half of the first inning with his second playoff home run. It was Pedroia's first World Series at-bat and he put the ball into the Monster seats in left. The Red Sox pounded Colorado starter Jeff Francis for six runs on 10 hits in four innings, then added seven more runs in the fifth and cruised to a 13–1 victory. The Rockies took it in stride and attributed it to being a bit rusty after having a record eight days off waiting for the ALCS to end.

Game 2 was a nail-biter. The Rockies pushed a run across in the first inning against Schilling on a Todd Helton groundout, and it stayed 1–0 until Jason Varitek's sacrifice fly in the fourth inning brought home Mike Lowell. In the fifth, Lowell drove home Ortiz with a double to left. The Red Sox led 2–1, but wouldn't score again. They needed their pitching to come through, and it did. Schilling lasted 5⅓ innings. Okajima came in with two runners on in the sixth and got out of the jam. He went 2⅓ innings, and then Papelbon got the final four outs, striking out Brad Hawpe to end the game. The Red Sox

> Fans celebrate Boston Red Sox pitcher Josh Beckett's strike-out against Colorado Rockies' Brad Hawpe in the fourth inning of Game 1 of the baseball World Series Wednesday, Oct. 24, 2007, at Fenway Park in Boston.
AP PHOTO/WINSLOW TOWNSON

had won their previous four games by a combined score of 43–6, but they survived Game 2 with a 2–1 victory.

The series moved to Coors Field in Colorado for Game 3, where the Red Sox bats came back to life. Ellsbury led the way with four hits, including three doubles and two RBIs. The Red Sox scored six times in the third inning, and took a 6–0 lead, but the Rockies battled back and Matt Holliday's three-run homer off Okajima in the seventh made it 6–5. The Red Sox responded with three runs in the top of the eighth, Ellsbury and Pedroia each hitting RBI doubles, and the Red Sox went on to finish with 15 hits and a 10–5 win. Matsuzaka pitched into the sixth inning and picked up his third win of the playoffs, and the Red Sox were on the verge of another World Series title.

With Tim Wakefield unavailable due to a shoulder injury, **the Red Sox handed**  **the ball to their young lefty, Jon Lester, who was making his first postseason start one year after undergoing chemotherapy.** Lester had thrown 3⅔ innings as a reliever in the Cleveland series, so he had already experienced the postseason, but he hadn't started a

> Boston Red Sox' Jon Lester pitches against the Colorado Rockies in the first inning of Game 4 of the baseball World Series Sunday, Oct. 28, 2007, at Coors Field in Denver. AP PHOTO/POOL, RICK WILKING

game in over a month. With a steely resolve, he went out and gave the Red Sox 5⅔ innings of shutout baseball. He gave up only three hits and got the series-clinching win!

The Red Sox scored runs in the first and fifth innings on base hits by David Ortiz and Jason Varitek, respectively, and Mike Lowell homered in the seventh inning to give the Red Sox a 3–0 lead. Colorado's Brad Hawpe answered with a solo home run of his own in the bottom of the seventh off Manny Delcarmen, and then Red Sox pinch-hitter Bobby Kielty's homer in the eighth proved to be the game winner, because Colorado's Garrett Atkins hit a two-run shot off Hideki Okajima to make it a 4–3 Red Sox lead. Jonathan Papelbon recorded the final five outs, the last one a strikeout of Seth Smith to earn his third save of the series. **The Red Sox were World Series champions for the second time in four years!** And as every Red Sox fan knows from the lyrics of "Sweet Caroline"—good times never seemed so good. So good. So good!

> The Boston Red Sox celebrate after the final out in Game 4 of the baseball World Series against the Colorado Rockies Sunday, Oct. 28, 2007, at Coors Field in Denver. The Red Sox won 4–3 to sweep the series.
AP PHOTO/DAVID J. PHILLIP

> Boston Red Sox pitcher Jonathan Papelbon, left, and catcher Jason Varitek celebrate after the Red Sox beat the Colorado Rockies, 4–3, to win the baseball World Series Sunday, Oct. 28, 2007, at Coors Field in Denver. AP PHOTO/DAVID ZALUBOWSKI

CHAPTER SIX

THE
2007–08 BOSTON CELTICS

Owner:
Wyc Grousbeck

General Manager:
Danny Ainge

Head Coach:
Doc Rivers

Regular Season Record:
53-21

Regular Season Finish:
First in Eastern Conference

Playoff Results:
Eastern Conference Quarterfinals—Boston
Celtics defeated Atlanta Hawks (4–3)

Eastern Conference Semifinals—Boston
Celtics defeated Cleveland Cavaliers (4–3)

Eastern Conference Finals—Boston Celtics
defeated Detroit Pistons (4–2)

NBA Finals:
Boston Celtics defeated
Los Angeles Lakers (4–2)

Awards:
NBA Finals MVP: F Paul Pierce

All-Stars: F Paul Pierce, F Kevin Garnett,
G Ray Allen

W ith the 10th pick in the 1998 NBA Draft, the Boston Celtics selected a junior out of the University of Kansas named Paul Pierce. He would be the first piece of the Celtics' new Big Three. Before the other two pieces were acquired, the Celtics would endure six losing seasons in Pierce's first nine seasons. The peak for the Celtics in those years would be reaching the Eastern Conference Finals in 2002, which was the team's first playoff appearance in seven years. The Celtics would make four straight playoff appearances, but they were a team moving in the wrong direction. Pierce would make five consecutive All-Star teams and earn the reputation as one of the most clutch players in the NBA, but the team around him wasn't very good, and by 2005, it was getting worse. The Celtics didn't make the playoffs that year, and when Pierce went down for seven weeks the following season with an injured left foot, the Celtics would set a franchise record with an 18-game losing streak and finish the year with the second worst record in the NBA.

To make matters worse, the Celtics missed on the chance to draft superstar-to-be Kevin Durant when they lost the NBA Draft Lottery and were assigned the fifth overall pick. Having

> Newly acquired Boston Celtics forward Kevin Garnett, center, stands with forward Paul Pierce, left, and guard Ray Allen during a news conference in this file photo taken July 31, 2007, in Boston. The addition of Garnett and Allen to team with Pierce make the Celtics a favorite in the Eastern Conference six months after finishing with the NBA's second worst record and 21 years after their last title.
AP PHOTO/STEVEN SENNE

won only 24 games in the 2006–07 season and then seeing the Ping-Pong balls go against them, this did not look like the beginning of the Celtics' 17th championship season. But it was!

On June 28, 2007, the night of the draft, the Celtics traded Delonte West, Wally Szczerbiak and the rights to their number 5 pick, Jeff Green, to the Seattle SuperSonics for seven-time All-Star Ray Allen and the SuperSonics' 35th overall pick, Glen Davis. **Allen was the second piece of the Celtics' new Big Three. It only took nine years to get him! And it only took 34 more days to get the third and final piece: Kevin Garnett.**

While the Red Sox were acquiring Eric Gagne on July 31, 2007, the Celtics were putting the finishing touches on the blockbuster deal that would bring Garnett to Boston. Eleven days earlier, the Celtics had met with Garnett and agreed to add three years and nearly $60 million to the two years left on his contract. Garnett was in line to make $104.9 million over the next five seasons playing in Boston. He just had to wait for Celtics president Danny Ainge to complete the deal with his longtime friend and former Celtics teammate, Timberwolves general manager Kevin McHale. Finally, McHale agreed. The Celtics would trade five players and two draft picks for Garnett, a 10-time All-Star and former NBA MVP. It would be a seven-for-one deal, making it the most number of players traded for one player in the history of the NBA. With the deal completed, the Celtics now had their new Big Three: Pierce, Allen, and Garnett.

Furthermore, a by-product of all of Ainge's wheeling and dealing was that he was left with second-year player Rajon Rondo as his starting point guard. The Celtics had acquired Rondo from the Phoenix Suns a year earlier, but Rondo spent his rookie season playing behind guards Delonte West and Sebastian Telfair. Both of them were included in the trades that brought Allen and Garnett to the Celtics, so Rondo would assume the pivotal role of getting the ball to the Big Three, and trying to make each of them happy.

Another by-product of Trader Danny's (Ainge) impulses was that the Celtics had only six returning players, and only two returning starters, Pierce and Kendrick Perkins. Left to put it all together was head coach Doc Rivers. To this point, Rivers was a well-respected coach, but not a successful one. In four years with the Orlando Magic, Rivers had been to the playoffs three times, but never advanced out of the first round. Hired by the Celtics in 2004, Rivers led the Celtics to the playoffs in his first season, but again lost in the first round when the Celtics dropped a seven-game series to the Indiana Pacers. Rivers had also presided over the Celtics' last two seasons in which they won only 33 and 24 games. There was certainly no guarantee that this creation of a new Big Three would work, but ultimately, it worked like a charm.

Garnett was welcomed to Boston by 36,000 screaming fans at Fenway Park when he threw out the ceremonial first pitch before the Red Sox—Orioles game the day after he was acquired by the Celtics. Three months later, he dazzled 18,000 more fans at the TD Garden as he filled up the stat sheet in his Celtics debut. Garnett's 22 points, 20 rebounds, five assists, three blocks, and three steals helped the Celtics beat the Milwaukee Bucks 103–83. This was certainly a great time to be a Boston sports fan. The Celtics made a huge statement that they were prepared to be a force to be reckoned with. Five days earlier, the Red Sox had won their second World Series in four years, and the Patriots were halfway through what would be an undefeated regular season and a fourth trip to the Super Bowl in eight years. Also each of the franchises was enjoying the others, and the fans loved to see that. Red Sox owner John Henry and Patriots owner Robert Kraft were both in attendance at the Celtics season opener. Henry and Red Sox president Larry Lucchino even brought the World Series trophy along with them, and there were several players from both the Red Sox and Patriots there as well.

> Newly acquired Boston Celtics forward Kevin Garnett pumps his fist after throwing out the ceremonial first pitch prior to a baseball game between the Boston Red Sox and the Baltimore Orioles at Fenway Park in Boston, Wednesday, Aug. 1, 2007. AP PHOTO/CHARLES KRUPA

The Celtics began the year with an eight-game winning streak, but they almost didn't make it two in a row. Their second game was against the Raptors in Toronto, and before the game, Doc Rivers learned that his father had passed away in Chicago. Rivers left to be with his family, and the Celtics were coached that night by assistant Tom Thibodeau. Toronto pushed the Celtics to overtime where Ray Allen won the game with a 3-pointer with less than three seconds to play.

The Celtics won their next five games by an average of 19 points, and then held a 15-point fourth quarter lead at home against the Miami Heat. They almost blew that game, but

The Big Three's Career Point Totals

Paul Pierce (26,397), Kevin Garnett (26,071) and Ray Allen (24,505) combined for 76,973 career points. They rank 15th, 17th, and 23rd, respectively.

> Boston Celtics forward Paul Pierce (34) puts up the game-winning shot over Miami Heat forward Udonis Haslem (40) in the final seconds of their basketball game in Boston, Friday, Nov. 16, 2007. The Celtics won 92–91 for their eighth consecutive win in their undefeated season. AP PHOTO/CHARLES KRUPA

> Boston Celtics' Kevin Garnett (5) muscles a rebound away from New York Knicks' Zach Randolph (50) during the first quarter of an NBA basketball game in Boston on Thursday, Nov. 29, 2007. AP PHOTO/ELISE AMENDOLA

Paul Pierce hit a driving layup with 25 seconds to play and the Celtics held on to win, 92–91. Two days later, the Celtics lost their first game of the season in Orlando.

"We didn't think we were going to go 82-0," Garnett said after the game. "But we are a team of character. We do play hard. We do play together, just not perfect."

The Celtics responded by winning 12 of their next 13 games, the one loss occurring at Cleveland against LeBron James and the Cavaliers. Ray Allen had a chance to put the Celtics ahead in the final minute of regulation, but uncharacteristically missed both free throws. The game went to overtime where James scored 11 of his 38 points, and the Celtics lost 109–104.

Among the wins was a 45-point drubbing of the New York Knicks. The 104–59 final was the sixth largest margin of victory in Celtics history. The Celtics also won a Friday night special at the Garden against the Los Angeles Lakers. The stars came out for this one. Arnold Schwarzenegger, his wife Maria Shriver, *Grey's Anatomy* star Ellen Pompeo, Richard Seymour of the Patriots, and former Celtic and Laker Rick Fox were all there to see what many believed could be a renewal of the Celtics-Lakers rivalry. The game was played with a playoff intensity, and the Celtics got 59 points from their Big Three and 21 more from Kendrick Perkins, and went on to win, 107–94.

The Celtics were playing as well as any Celtics team in the history of the storied franchise. On December 14, they beat the Milwaukee Bucks and improved to 12-0 at home, matching the start of the 1984 Celtics who went on to win the NBA title. **Two nights later, they beat the Toronto Raptors to improve to 20-2**, equaling the record of the 1963 Celtics, who went on to win the NBA title. There was a long way to go, but the Celtics looked like a team that could raise the 17th championship banner in team history.

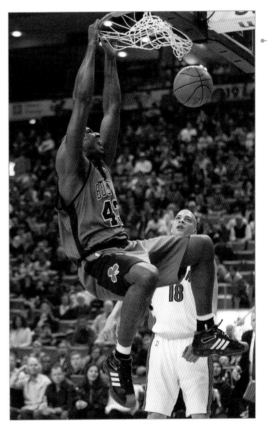

There was a slight stumble at home against the Pistons on December 19. Detroit's Chauncey Billups hit a pair of free throws with a 10th of a second remaining in regulation, and the Celtics lost their first home game of the season, 87–85. The Celtics then ran off another nine straight wins, including each game of a four-game West Coast road trip. When they beat the Seattle SuperSonics, their record stood at 24-3. It was a startling turnaround from the previous season when the Celtics won a total of 24 games, and finished 24-58.

During the nine-game winning streak, the Celtics won at the Lakers, thereby sweeping the season series, and then avenged their

> Toronto Raptors forward Anthony Parker (18) watches as Boston Celtics center Kendrick Perkins, top, slams home a dunk during first-half NBA basketball action in Toronto, Canada, on Sunday, Dec. 16, 2007. AP PHOTO/THE CANADIAN PRESS,FRANK GUNN

loss to the Pistons by winning 92–85 in Detroit. **Against the → Pistons, Glen "Big Baby" Davis led the Celtics with a career-high 20 points. It was the first time all year that someone other than Pierce, Garnett, or Allen led the Celtics in scoring, and if the Celtics needed a confidence boost, they got it.**

"This was a huge win," Pierce said, "because we won on the road in a playoff atmosphere against a team that had won 11 straight."

So, the Celtics were 29-3, and their three losses were by two points twice and once in overtime. They were the elite team in the league, and everything was going right. And then they lost three out of four and went just 7-6 during a surprisingly mediocre stretch. They lost at home to the Charlotte Bobcats, who came to Boston with a 1-11 road record. They

▸ Boston Celtics forward Glen Davis (11) shoots over the defense of Detroit Pistons forward Rasheed Wallace (36) during the second quarter of an NBA basketball game at the Palace of Auburn Hills, Mich., Saturday, Jan. 5, 2008. Davis scored a career-high 20 points, giving Boston's Big Three a huge lift in a 92–85 win. AP PHOTO/CARLOS OSORIO

lost back-to-back games to the Washington Wizards. **They lost in Orlando on Hedo —— Türkoglu's buzzer-beating 3-pointer, 96–93.** And they lost for the second time to LeBron James and the Cavaliers.

After the loss to the Cavs, the Celtics rebounded with a five-game winning streak, and headed into the All-Star break with a 41-9 record. They were a perfect 16-0 against the Western Conference, but that streak was snapped immediately coming out of the break. Despite Garnett

> Orlando Magic forward Hedo Turkoglu, center, of Turkey, is swarmed by teammates after hitting the game-winning basket over the Boston Celtics as time ran out of their basketball game in Orlando, Fla., Sunday, Jan. 27, 2008. The Magic won, 96–93.
AP PHOTO/PHELAN M. EBENHACK

returning after missing nine straight games with an abdominal strain, the Celtics lost three straight games at Denver, Golden State, and Phoenix. The Celtics wrapped up the road trip with wins at Phoenix against the Suns and newly acquired Shaquille O'Neal, and at Los Angeles against the Clippers. They then added eight more consecutive wins to give them a 10-game winning streak, their longest in 22 years.

" This is the number one team in the league," Brown told the Boston Globe, "and these All-Star guys say, 'We think you can help us.' Coming from a player? When you hear from players, guys that are in the trenches, guys who have busted their tails to make their team where it is up to this point, it really meant a lot. **"**

> Boston Celtics' Sam Cassell, right, pass the ball as Philadelphia 76ers' Shavlik Randolph during the third quarter of an NBA basketball game Monday, March 10, 2008, in Philadelphia. AP PHOTO/H. RUMPH, JR.

During the winning streak, the Celtics signed a pair of 38-year-olds: P. J. Brown and Sam Cassell. Brown, a 6'11" power forward, had played in the NBA for 14 seasons before going into semi-retirement. He was living in Louisiana and was in New Orleans for All-Star Weekend, which is where Paul Pierce saw him walking across Canal Street.

"P. J., we could use you!" Pierce shouted out his car window. Two nights later, Pierce and Allen ran into Brown at a party and convinced him to sign with the Celtics.

Cassell was a 15-year veteran who had convinced the Clippers to buy him out of his contract so he could sign with a contending team. Cassell hadn't played in two weeks because of an injured wrist, but he brought the Celtics a much-needed backup to Rajon Rondo at point guard, and he brought them much-needed playoff experience. Cassell had already played in 115 playoff games during his 15-year career, and won two championship rings with the Houston Rockets. Before his signing, the only Celtic with a ring was James Posey, who won his two years earlier with the Miami Heat. The Celtics were Cassell's eighth team, and reunited him with Allen and with Garnett, whom he had played with in Milwaukee and Minnesota, respectively.

"We're just going to wait and see where he fits in on our team," Rivers said. "He's coming in with the right frame of mind, and he just wants to help. He knows how to play. He's terrific at the end of games. He can still really play."

> Boston Celtics' Kevin Garnett (5) goes up to dunk the ball as Houston Rockets' Luis Scola (4), of Argentina, defends during the fourth quarter of a basketball game Tuesday, March 18, 2008, in Houston. The Rockets' 22-game win streak ended as the Celtics beat the Rockets 94–74. AP PHOTO/BOB LEVEY

Cassell made his Celtics debut on March 10 against Philadelphia when the Celtics extended their winning streak to nine games and won their 50th game in a season for the first time in 16 years. Brown debuted the next night, as the Celtics won easily over a bad Seattle SuperSonics team, but the Celtics' 10-game winning streak was snapped at home against the Utah Jazz. Ray Allen jammed his left ankle in the first quarter of that game, and would miss the next three games, all Celtics victories. **Without Allen, the Celtics won at San Antonio, then ended the Houston Rockets' 22-game winning streak,** which was the second longest in NBA history, and then with Allen back in the lineup, the Celtics won at Dallas for the first time in eight years.

> Boston Celtics forward Paul Pierce, center, laughs with teammates Ray Allen, left, and forward Kevin Garnett, right, during a timeout in the second half of their NBA basketball game against the New Jersey Nets in Boston, Wednesday, April 16, 2008. The Celtics beat the Nets 105–94. AP PHOTO/CHARLES KRUPA

The Celtics were 51-13 and ready for the stretch run. As long as they had their Big Three, the Celtics had proven over the course of the regular season that they could not only beat anyone, but they could dominate on any given night. So, over the course of the final 18 games, head coach Doc Rivers reduced the minutes of Pierce, Garnett, and Allen, and sat them out of a few games completely. Even so, the Celtics went 15-3 to close out the season. They finished with 66 wins, third most in franchise history, and with the best record in the NBA, they had earned home court advantage throughout the playoffs. Before their final game of the season on April 16 against the New Jersey Nets, **Pierce grabbed a microphone and addressed the TD Garden crowd.**

"All I can remember the last two or three years is promising you all better days," Pierce said. "We've got better days now! We want to make this a great year. In order for us to do that, we need to get another banner up in these rafters."

Four days later, the Celtics opened their first playoff series in three years with a 23-point blowout win over the eighth-seeded Atlanta Hawks, who had gone just 37-45 in the regular

> Boston Celtics' Kevin Garnett, right, blocks a shot attempt by the New Jersey Nets' Sean Williams during the second quarter of an NBA basketball game Friday night, Jan. 11, 2008, in East Rutherford, N.J. AP PHOTO/BILL KOSTROUN

> Atlanta Hawks forward Josh Smith (5) goes up for a shot while Boston Celtics guard Rajon Rondo (9) and forward Paul Pierce (34) watch during the first quarter of Game 3 of the NBA basketball first-round playoff series, Saturday, April 26, 2008, in Atlanta. AP PHOTO/STANLEY LEARY

season. The Celtics then won Game 2 by 19 points. The Celtics dominated the first two games with great defense that held the Hawks to an average of 79 points, and with a balanced offense. No Celtic scored as many as 20 points in the first two games. **Meanwhile, on the Tuesday between Games 1 and 2, Kevin Garnett was named the NBA's Defensive Player of the Year for helping the Celtics hold opponents to the lowest field goal percentage in the league.**

The series moved to Atlanta for Games 3 and 4, and that's where the Celtics discovered they were in for a fight, almost literally. The Hawks won the third game, 103–92, behind 27 points from Josh Smith. **He had five dunks in the game, including one especially electrifying rim-rocker over Ray Allen that put the Hawks ahead by 12 points with 7:39 to play.** Hawks rookie forward Al Horford had 17 points and 14 rebounds, and a memorably testy exchange with Paul Pierce in the final minute. Pierce had fallen down while Horford hit a jump shot, and while Pierce was still on one knee, Horford went

right up to him and shouted in his face. That prompted Pierce to walk over toward the Hawks' bench and make what the NBA later determined was a "menacing gesture." Pierce was fined $25,000 for what may have been a gang sign with his right hand, though Pierce denies that's what it was.

Game 4 was equally feisty, and the Celtics lost again, 97–92. In the second quarter, Garnett went for a loose ball and threw an elbow at Zaza Pachulia. Those two went forehead to forehead and had to be separated before any punches were thrown. The Celtics led by 10 going into the fourth quarter, but missed nine of their first 10 shots in the period. Atlanta's Joe Johnson scored 20 of his game-high 35 points in the fourth quarter, and Josh Smith chipped in with 28 points and seven blocked shots. The series was suddenly tied 2–2.

"We've got to find ourselves real quick," Cassell said after the game. "We've got to find our team identity, our team chemistry. We've got to find all that real quick."

The Celtics went back to Boston and won Game 5 by 25 points, 110–85. The formula once again was a stifling defense that held Atlanta without a field goal for over seven minutes in the first half, and balanced scoring. Pierce led the way with 22 points. Garnett had 20, and Allen had 19. It was the Celtics' third blowout victory at home, but they led the series only 3–2. And then they returned to Atlanta for Game 6, and lost again. The 66-win Celtics were pushed to a Game 7 by the worst team to make the playoffs.

Game 6 came down to the final minute. Joe Johnson hit a huge 3-pointer over James Posey to put the Hawks up 100–95. Posey responded with a 3-pointer of his own with 48 seconds remaining. Ray Allen had a chance to take the lead in the closing seconds, but missed from beyond the arc, and then Rondo missed a desperation three that would have forced overtime as time expired. For the third time in the series, the Hawks and their

Most Wins in a Celtics Season

The Celtics franchise record for wins in a season is 68 set in 1972–73, but they lost the Eastern Conference Finals that year to the New York Knicks in seven games.

> Boston Celtics forward Kevin Garnett (5) pulls on his shirt and yells as the Celtics take a commanding lead in the second half of Game 7 of an NBA first-round playoff basketball series against the Atlanta Hawks in Boston, Sunday, May 4, 2008. The Celtics defeated the Hawks 99–65. AP PHOTO/CHARLES KRUPA

fans celebrated as if they had just won the NBA title. After each victory, streamers fell from the ceiling of Philips Arena. Pachulia grabbed then-Hawks TV sideline reporter Rashan Ali's microphone and shouted to the crowd, "Nothing easy! We're going to Game 7, baby! Game 7! Game 7!"

The Hawks lost Game 7 by 34 points! The series had been surprisingly difficult, but Game 7 was easy. The Celtics rolled to a 99–65 final. They scored 27 points in the first quarter. The Hawks scored 26 points in the first half. While the Celtics lead was ballooning to 38 points in the third quarter, **Garnett made an emphatic dunk and then turned to the crowd, slashed his hand across his throat, and said, "It's over."**

Two days later, it began all over again: a seven-game series in which the home team won every game. This time the opponent was LeBron James and the Cleveland Cavaliers. The stars did not come out for Game 1. James scored 12 points on 2-of-18 shooting. Pierce had a career playoff low four points and was 2-for-14 from the field. Allen missed the only four shots he took and was held scoreless for the first time in 852 games. The only star that shone was Garnett, who led all scorers with 28 points, and the Celtics took the first game, 76–72. James had a

> Cleveland Cavaliers' LeBron James, second from right, yells at his mother, Gloria, left, who left her seat after a foul on James by Boston Celtics' Paul Pierce, second from left, in the second quarter of Game 4 of the NBA basketball Eastern Conference semifinals Monday, May 12, 2008, in Cleveland. The Boston Celtics' Kevin Garnett is on the right. AP PHOTO/MARK DUNCAN

chance to tie the game with 8.5 seconds left, but missed a layup. In fact, he missed his last six shots in Game 1, and then missed his first three shots in Game 2. The Celtics won the second game as well, 89–73, and James went back to Cleveland having shot 8-for-42 in Boston.

James was better in Game 3, but not by much. He had 21 points on 5-of-16 shooting, making him 13-for-58 in the first three games. He was shooting 22.4 percent from the field, which was the worst of any three-game playoff stretch in 30 years, but the Cavaliers won Game 3, 108–84. That's because the Cavaliers not named LeBron James shot 59 percent, and pulled out to a 19-point lead in the first quarter, and rode that to a 24-point victory.

"It's probably the worst game we've played since I've been a part of the Celtics," Cassell said. "Unfortunately, it came at the wrong time. We've got to regroup and get our swagger back."

That didn't happen in Game 4. The Celtics lost again, 88–77, scoring just 12 points in the fourth quarter. The game included **a moment where Pierce and James tumbled together into the seats under the basket right where James's mother, Gloria, was sitting.** She jumped up and shouted at Pierce, and LeBron tried to calm his

> Cleveland Cavaliers' LeBron James (23) dunks on Boston Celtics' Kevin Garnett in the final two minutes of Game 4 of the NBA basketball Eastern Conference semifinals Monday, May 12, 2008, in Cleveland. The Cavaliers beat Boston 88–77 to even the series at 2-2. AP PHOTO/TONY DEJAK

mother down. That was fun, but the signature moment in the game and the series occurred with 1:45 remaining. **James drove by Pierce and dunked the ball over Garnett.** It was one of those powerful and posterizing dunks that energize a team and a crowd. The play was shown repeatedly on the video board at Quicken Loans Arena. Each time, the crowd gasped and erupted. The Celtics, who were an NBA best 31-10 on the road during the regular season, had now lost all five road playoff games, and were headed back to Boston with the series tied 2–2.

Back home meant back to winning for the Celtics. Pierce had 29 points in Game 5. Garnett had 26 points and 16 rebounds, and Rondo had 20 points with 13 assists. James was hot early, but missed 10 of his last 14 shots, including all five 3-point attempts. His 35-point effort wasn't enough as the Celtics won, 96–89. The difference was at the free throw line where the Cavaliers missed ten times in the second half, and Pierce made five of six in the final 15 seconds to seal the deal.

The Celtics held the Cavaliers to just 74 points in Game 6, but only managed to score 69 points themselves. It was the second-lowest point total in Celtics playoff history. James had 32 points to lead the Cavaliers. Garnett had 25, but once again the Celtics lost on the road.

"Mentally we feel like we're a confident team," Pierce said. "We've been in Game 7s before, and we feel like this is a game we let slip away. Hopefully, we can go home and take care of business."

They did. **Game 7 will be remembered as an epic battle between Pierce and James**, each man attempting to will his team to victory. Pierce's will won out! With Patriot players Tom Brady, Richard Seymour, Vince Wilfork, Kevin Faulk, and Laurence Maroney on hand to witness, James finished with 45 points to Pierce's 41, but the Celtics prevailed, 97–92.

The game went down to the wire, and with 2:20 left, James stole the ball from Pierce and raced down the length of the floor. His thunderous dunk cut the Celtics' lead to 89–88, but after that James missed a 3-pointer, a five-footer, and a free throw, and the Celtics advanced with a 4–3 series victory. They were the first team to advance through the second round without a road win. They would face the Detroit Pistons in the Eastern Conference Finals.

The Pistons had finished off the Orlando Magic in five games and had

▸ Boston Celtics forward Paul Pierce (34) blocks Cleveland Cavaliers forward LeBron James (23) in Game 7 of an NBA Eastern Conference semifinal basketball series in Boston on Sunday, May 18, 2008.
AP PHOTO/CHARLES KRUPA

six days to rest before the start of the finals. The Celtics had just one day to prepare for the Pistons, but they still managed to win their 15th straight home game, 88–79. Garnett and Pierce combined for 48 points, and a stifling Celtic's defense held Detroit to just 17 third quarter points. Trouble didn't come until Game 2, when the Celtics were finally beaten at home. The home court advantage they had earned with 66 regular-season victories was suddenly gone. Game 2 featured another solid contribution from Garnett and Pierce, who combined for 50 points, and Ray Allen finally broke out of his shooting slump with 25 points, but the Celtics lost 103–97. Allen's 3-pointer with five minutes to play cut the Pistons lead to 88–86, and another 3-pointer with 10 seconds to go made it a three-point deficit, 100–97, but Detroit made its free throws in the final seconds and evened the series at one game apiece.

The Celtics finally broke through with a road victory in Game 3. They raced out to an 18-point halftime lead, held on to it through three quarters, and went on to win, 94–80. That's more like it!

"I think the loss rejuvenated us," said Pierce. "We really wanted to come out and get this one."

And it showed, but stepping into the rejuvenation machine for Game 4 was the Pistons' Antonio McDyess. The 33-year-old had his best game of the playoffs with 21 points and 16 rebounds, and the Pistons once again evened the series with a convincing 94–75 win.

Back home for Game 5, the Celtics' Big Three finally put it all together, and they got a lot of help from Kendrick Perkins. Garnett led the way with 33 points. Allen had a career playoff high 29 points, and Pierce added 16, but it was Perkins's 18 points and 16 rebounds that made the biggest difference.

"Perkins is eating us up," said Pistons head coach Flip Saunders.

The Celtics began the fourth quarter with a 17-point lead, but when Rodney Stuckey stuck a 3-pointer with 1:23 to go, the Celtics lead was just 100–99. Allen hit a long jumper to give the Celtics a three-point lead, and Garnett secured the 106–102 win with a couple of free throws in the final seconds.

In Game 6 at The Palace of Auburn Hills, the Celtics trailed by 10 points early in the fourth quarter, but rode a 19–4 surge to an 89–81 victory. With 5:30 to go, Pierce drove to the basket and made a spinning layup to

› Boston Celtics' Kendrick Perkins, right, goes to the basket past Detroit Pistons' Chauncey Billups during the second half of Game 5 of the NBA Eastern Conference basketball finals in Boston, Wednesday, May 28, 2008.
AP PHOTO/WINSLOW TOWNSON

tie the game, 74–74. He was fouled on the play and made the free throw to give the Celtics a lead they would never relinquish. Pierce scored the game's next four points and would finish with a game-high 27. The Celtics were headed to their first appearance in the NBA Finals since 1987. The 1987 appearance was part of a run in which the Celtics went to the Finals four years in a row, and in three of those years, they squared off against the Los Angeles Lakers. This year they would be facing the Lakers once again. As it should be!

Game 1 of the 2008 NBA Finals will forever be remembered as the "Wheelchair Game." Midway through the third quarter, Perkins fell into the back of Pierce's right knee. Pierce was in excruciating pain, and said later he felt a "pop" in the knee. He writhed on the floor for several minutes before being carried off the Garden parquet by Brian Scalabrine and

> Boston Celtics forward Paul Pierce (34) is carried from the court by teammates Brian Scalabrine, back left, and Tony Allen, right, after an injury in the third quarter during Game 1 of the NBA basketball finals against the Los Angeles Lakers in Boston, Thursday, June 5, 2008. AP PHOTO/CHARLES KRUPA

Tony Allen. Pierce was taken to the locker room in a wheelchair, and there was concern his season could be over. That concern didn't last long, however. About three minutes later, Pierce returned to the court and finished off a 15-point third quarter by knocking down a couple of 3-pointers and helping the Celtics to a 77–73 lead.

"I think God just sent this angel down and said, 'Hey, you're going to be all right,'" Pierce said after the game. 'You need to get back out there. Show them what you've got.'"

Pierce's dramatic return along with his 22 points helped the Celtics to a 98–88 win, and despite what was diagnosed as a strained knee, Pierce led the Celtics with 28 points in Game 2. The Celtics won again, 108–102, but this one will be remembered as the game in which the Celtics almost blew a 24-point fourth quarter lead. The Lakers scored 41 points in the fourth quarter, and a couple of free throws by Kobe Bryant with 38 seconds to play made it a 104–102 Celtics lead.

Pierce and James Posey made their free throws down the stretch, and Pierce partially blocked a 3-point attempt by Sasha Vujačić. The Celtics escaped the near collapse and took a 2–0 series lead to Los Angeles.

Ray Allen was 8-for-13 in Game 3, but Pierce and Garnett were just 8-for-35. Pierce, playing near his childhood home of Inglewood, California, had averaged 25 points in the first two games, but scored only six in Game 3. The Celtics led by two after three quarters and held on to that lead until the 6:54 mark of the fourth quarter. That's when Bryant took a little extra time and knocked down a three that gave the Lakers a 69–68 lead. Bryant finished with 36 points, and the Lakers went on to win, 87–81.

> Boston Celtics guard Eddie House celebrates after the Celtics beat the Los Angeles Lakers 97–91 in Game 4 of the NBA basketball finals Thursday, June 12, 2008, in Los Angeles. AP PHOTO/MARK J. TERRILL

The Lakers entered Game 4 with a 15-game winning streak at the Staples Center, but the series turned when **the Celtics erased a 24-point deficit and shocked the Lakers with the largest comeback in the NBA Finals since 1971.**

"It's definitely a great win," Pierce said, "one that you're going to put up there in the library and break back out one day for your kids to watch, but I want nothing more than that ring right now."

Without the benefit of a single point from Bryant, the Lakers took a 35–14 first quarter lead, and expanded the margin in the second quarter when Vujačić nailed a 3-pointer to make it 45–21. The Celtics were still down by 20 with seven minutes to go in the third, but they closed out the quarter with a 21–3 run. Eddie House hit a couple of 3-pointers and P. J. Brown closed out the quarter with a monster dunk that cut the Laker lead to 73–71.

The Celtics took their first lead of the game on a House jumper with 4:07 remaining, and Allen followed that with a sweet reverse layup to make it 86–83 Celtics. They went on to win Game 4, 97–91, taking a commanding 3–1 lead in the series.

No NBA team had ever come back to win a series after trailing 3–1. Twenty-eight had tried, and 28 had failed. The Lakers would be number 29, but they did manage to push the series

Team Pride

❝ They don't hang up any other banners but championship ones," Pierce said. "And now I'm a part of it. And just all the years talking to Bill and John, Cousy, finally I feel like we've come out of that shadow now and created our own. Now we can stand up and look them eye to eye and say, 'Hey, we accomplished it, too.' ❞

> Boston Celtics Hall of Fame center Bill Russell, left, walks off the court with Kevin Garnett after the Celtics won the 2008 NBA basketball championship with a 131–92 win over the Los Angeles Lakers on Tuesday, June 17, 2008, in Boston. AP PHOTO/WINSLOW TOWNSON

back to Boston. In Game 5, the Celtics dug themselves another hole and this time couldn't climb out of it. They trailed by 19 in the second quarter, but battled back and closed the gap to 55–52 at halftime. The biggest play of the game came with the Lakers leading by two with 45 seconds remaining. Pierce, who had a game-high 38 points, pulled down a rebound and dribbled toward the hoop. He could have tied the game, but Bryant reached around and poked the ball away. Lamar Odom grabbed the ball and fed it to Bryant, who raced down the floor and slammed an emphatic two-handed dunk. The Lakers went on to win Game 5, 103–98.

To this point in the series, every game was decided by 10 points or fewer. So, it came as a bit of a surprise when the Celtics closed out the series with a 39-point blowout win in Game 6. What was expected to be a bitter battle to the end quickly became a coronation. The Celtics grabbed a 23-point halftime lead and refused to let it slip away as it had in Game 2.

Garnett and Allen each had 26 points. Rondo blossomed with 21 points, eight assists, and six steals. And Pierce, who won the Finals MVP award, scored 17. **With Bill Russell, John Havlicek, Tommy Heinsohn, and other Celtic's legends witnessing firsthand, the Celtics earned their 17th championship banner with a 131–92 win.**

> Boston Celtics' Kevin Garnett, left, Ray Allen, center, and Paul Pierce celebrate in the locker room after winning the NBA basketball championship with a 131–92 win over the Los Angeles Lakers on Tuesday, June 17, 2008, in Boston. AP PHOTO/WINSLOW TOWNSON

Doc Rivers pulled Pierce, Garnett, and Allen out of the game with 4:01 to play. All four group-hugged and thanked each other for this special moment. When the game was over, **Garnett knelt down and kissed the Celtics leprechaun logo at midcourt.**

"This is the reason we came here," he said. "This is the reason we got together."

Danny Ainge brought them together. Doc Rivers held it together. And the Big Three got it done—together.

> Boston Celtics forward Kevin Garnett kisses the Boston Celtics logo as he celebrates the Celtics' 131–92 win over the Los Angeles Lakers to win the NBA basketball Championship in Boston, Tuesday, June 17, 2008. AP PHOTO/CHARLES KRUPA

CHAPTER SEVEN

THE
2010–11 BOSTON BRUINS

Owner:
Jeremy Jacobs

General Manager:
Peter Chiarelli

Head Coach:
Claude Julien

Regular Season Record:
46-25-11

Regular Season Finish:
First in Northeast Division

Playoff Results:
Conference Quarterfinals—Boston Bruins
defeated
Montreal Canadiens (4–3)

Conference Semifinals—Boston Bruins
defeated
Philadelphia Flyers (4–0)

Conference Finals—Boston Bruins defeated
Tampa Bay Lightning (4–3)

Stanley Cup Finals:
Boston Bruins defeated
Vancouver Canucks (4–3

Awards:
Finals MVP: G Tim Thomas

All-Stars: D Zdeno Chára, G Tim Thomas,
F Milan Lucic

So, as we count the rings, the total was up to six in eight years with the Patriots winning three, the Red Sox two, and the Celtics one. It was time for the Bruins to step up! They hadn't won the Stanley Cup since 1972, and the way their 2009–10 season ended, they didn't look like prime candidates to win it again. After finishing last in the league in goals scored, the Bruins managed to advance to the Eastern Conference Semifinals, where they blew a 3–0 series lead and a 3–0 Game 7 lead against the Flyers. It was one of the worst playoff collapses in any sport—ever! The shocking and sudden ending to the season had the Bruins scrambling to find answers.

The first thing they did was promote Cam Neely and name him team president on June 16, 2010. A week later, they traded defenseman Dennis Wideman to the Florida Panthers for productive winger Nathan Horton. In the deal the Bruins also got center Gregory Campbell and gave up their 15th overall pick in the NHL Draft. Horton was drafted third overall in 2003, and had scored at least 20 goals in five straight seasons.

The Bruins could afford to give up the 15th pick in the draft, because they also had the second overall pick, which they had

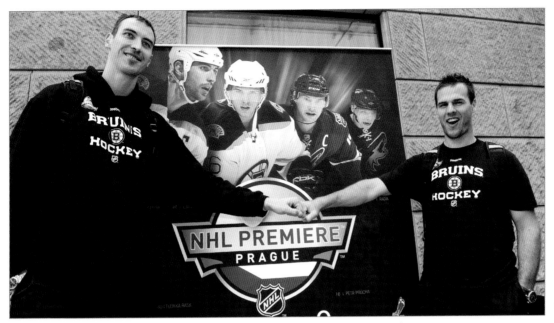

> NHL hockey team Boston Bruins Slovak player Zdeno Chara, left, and his Czech team-mate David Krejčí, right, pose in front of a poster after arriving in Prague on Sunday, Oct. 3, 2010. AP PHOTO,CTK, KATERINA SULOVA

acquired in the Phil Kessel trade the previous September with the Toronto Maple Leafs. Kessel had 60 points in 70 games for the Bruins as a 21-year-old center in 2008–09, but he rejected a four-year, $16 million contract offer in July, and was traded to the Leafs for two first-round draft picks and a second rounder. Kessel immediately signed a five-year, $27 million contract with Toronto. So, the deal was good for him, and it looked a lot better for the Bruins when the Leafs finished with the second-worst record in the NHL, thus giving the Bruins the number 2 pick. So, days after the Horton trade, the Bruins added talented 18-year-old center Tyler Seguin to the roster. Seguin had tallied 106 points in 63 games with the OHL's Plymouth Whalers.

Before the start of the season, the Bruins also re-signed 25-year-old center Patrice Bergeron to a three-year, $15 million extension, and rewarded 2009 Norris Trophy winner Zdeno Chára with a seven-year, $45.5 million extension. Bergeron and Chára, along with a corps that included Marc Savard, David Krejčí, and Milan Lucic, were part of the Bruins team that had earned 116 points in the regular season in 2008–09. Now, with the additions of Horton, Seguin, and Campbell, and the potential development of second-year player Brad Marchand, there was optimism surrounding the Bruins, but there weren't many who predicted what was about to unfold.

The Bruins began the 2010–11 season in Prague, Czech Republic, with two games against the Phoenix Coyotes.

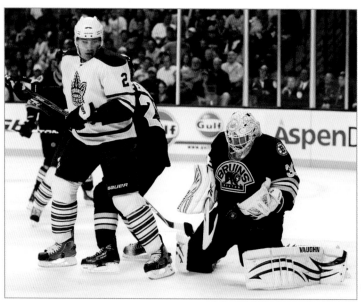

> Boston Bruins goalie Tim Thomas makes a save as Toronto Maple Leafs' Luke Schenn looks for the rebound during the first period of an NHL hockey game in Boston on Thursday, Oct. 28, 2010. AP PHOTO/WINSLOW TOWNSON

The Half-Century Mark

C am Neely scored 50 goals in 49 games during the 1993–94 season. He scored at least 50 goals three times in his 13-year NHL career.

Tuukka Rask, who had led the NHL in goals-against average and save percentage as a rookie the previous year, started the season opener and lost. Thirty-six-year-old Tim Thomas, who had led the NHL in those same categories and won the Vezina Trophy in 2008–09, started the next four games and won them all. **Thomas began the year as the backup to Rask, but quickly reclaimed his starting position.** He won his first eight starts, giving up just nine goals and earning three shutouts in the process. He was 10-1 before Rask shutout the Florida Panthers for his first win of the year on November 18.

Thomas recorded his fifth shutout at Philadelphia on December 1, and then came home to beat Tampa Bay, 8–1, in the Bruins' highest-scoring game of the year. It was the Bruins' 23rd game, but Marc Savard's first. He'd been out for the last month of the previous regular season with a concussion, and he scored in his first game back. Lucic was among the seven

> Boston Bruins' Shawn Thornton, left, and Dallas Stars' Krys Barch fight during the first period of an NHL hockey game in Boston on Thursday, Feb. 3, 2011. AP PHOTO/WINSLOW TOWNSON

Bruins who scored against the Lightning. It was his 12th goal of the year, three more than his total from the previous season.

After a 5–2 win over the New York Islanders, the Bruins hit a mid-December slump, losing four of five games and falling into eighth place in the Eastern Conference. They were 17-11-4, but barely holding on to a playoff spot. They responded by winning three in a row and picking up 21 points in their next 14 games. During the stretch, Patrice Bergeron recorded his first career hat trick in a 6–0 win over the Ottawa Senators; Zdeno Chára recorded his first career hat trick in a 7–0 win over the Carolina Hurricanes; Tim Thomas went 7-0-3; and the Bruins moved into first place in the Northeast Division.

The Bruins held that position into the All-Star break, but along the way they lost Marc Savard. His career ended on January 22 at Colorado when his former teammate, Matt Hunwick, made a legal hit on him in the corner. It was a routine check into the boards, but Savard suffered the sixth and final concussion of his career. He explained to the *Boston Globe* later that he saw pitch black with his eyes open and was "quite scared." He would never play again.

The Bruins returned from the All-Star break ready to fight. In their second game they hosted the Dallas Stars, and there were three fights in the first four seconds!

Stars instigator Steve Ott squared off with Gregory Campbell as soon as the puck dropped. Campbell was bloodied in that battle. So, immediately upon the second puck drop, the Bruins' Shawn Thornton pounded Stars forward Krys Barch. And then, why not? Adam McQuaid and Brian Sutherby dropped the gloves. The fights ignited the Bruins more than the Stars as Marchand and Bergeron each scored in the game's first 80 seconds. There were a total of four fights and 91 penalty minutes in the game, and the Bruins went on to win, 6–3.

Six nights later, the Bruins beat the Montreal Canadiens, 8–6, in a game that featured 45 penalties for a total of 187 penalty minutes, including two fighting majors for the goaltenders. The craziness began in the second period after the Bruins took a 5–3 lead on a Lucic goal. Five seconds after the ensuing faceoff, a skirmish developed behind the Montreal goal. While the players pushed and pulled at each other, Tim Thomas suddenly sprinted out of his crease and raced down the ice to challenge Montreal goaltender Carey Price to a fight. The referee let them go, and Price quickly put Thomas gently onto the ice, and the two men ended up smiling about the altercation. However, in the game's final minute, four fights occurred simultaneously. At this point in the season, the Bruins led the NHL with 55 fight majors in 54 games.

The win over the Canadiens increased the Bruins' division lead to four points, but they lost their next three games. At the end of the slump, the Bruins traded their second-round pick to the Ottawa Senators for center Chris Kelly. A couple of nights later, they acquired

> Montreal Canadiens goalie Carey Price (31) fights with Boston Bruins goalie Tim Thomas (30) during the second period of an NHL hockey game in Boston, Wednesday, Feb. 9, 2011.
AP PHOTO/ELISE AMENDOLA

center Rich Peverley and defenseman Boris Valábik in a trade that sent Blake Wheeler and Mark Stuart to the Atlanta Thrashers. And in a third deal with the Toronto Maple Leafs, the Bruins gave up top prospect Joe Colborne, their first-round pick in the 2011 draft, and a conditional pick to acquire well-respected defenseman Tomáš Kaberle, who had 38 points in 58 games with the Leafs that season. The Bruins were clearly going for it!

"We felt that we needed a player like Tomáš," Bruins GM Peter Chiarelli said, "A player with good vision, a good skater who can quarterback a power play and has played many, many games in the league. It was an important piece for us to get, and obviously, we had to pay a price."

Kaberle would contribute a goal and eight assists in 24 regular-season games with the Bruins, which may not have been up to expectations, but he also would chip in with 11 assists in the Bruins' 25 playoff games.

During this trading frenzy, the Bruins embarked upon a six-game road trip that began on Long Island and made two stops in Ottawa. **The Bruins won all six games, outscoring their opponents 20–9.** The only other time a Bruins team enjoyed a 6-0 road

> Boston Bruins' Milan Lucic, left, celebrates his goal with teammate Nathan Horton during the first period of an NHL hockey game against the Calgary Flames in Calgary, Alberta, Tuesday, Feb. 22, 2011. AP PHOTO/THE CANADIAN PRESS, JEFF MCINTOSH

> In this March 8, 2011, file photo, Montreal Canadiens' Max Pacioretty is checked by Boston Bruins' Zdeno Chára during second-period NHL hockey action in Montreal. Montreal Police have completed their investigation into Chára for his hit on Pacioretty, forwarding the report to prosecutors. Crown lawyers will decide whether to charge Boston's captain for the hit that sidelined Pacioretty with a concussion and a cracked vertebra. AP PHOTO/THE CANADIAN PRESS, PAUL CHIASSON

trip was back in 1972, the last time the Bruins won the Stanley Cup. It was a very good sign, and the Bruins won their seventh in a row when they returned home and beat the Tampa Bay Lightning, 2–1. That victory lifted the Bruins into sole possession of second place in the Eastern Conference, three points behind the Philadelphia Flyers. The Bruins then went on to lose four straight and six of their next seven.

The inexplicable slump included a particularly memorable game at Montreal on March 8. With 15.8 seconds remaining in the second period, Zdeno Chára checked Max Pacioretty into the glass partition at the end of the Bruins' bench. If the check had been done anywhere else on the ice, it would have been a harmless hit, but Pacioretty went headfirst into the padded stanchion supporting the glass partition and crumpled to the ice. He lay motionless for a few minutes before being taken off the ice on a stretcher. **Pacioretty suffered a severe concussion and a cracked vertebra.**

"Obviously, that wasn't my intention to push him into the post," explained Chára. "It's very unfortunate. In that situation everything's happening fast, and even planning to do that, that's not my style to hurt somebody. I always play hard. I play physical, but I never try to hurt anybody. So, I'm hoping he's okay."

Chára was given an interference major and a game misconduct for the hit, but was not suspended. And that upset Pacioretty.

"I would feel better if he (Chára) said he made a mistake," Pacioretty said, "and that he was sorry for doing that. I could forgive that. I believe he was trying to guide my head into the turnbuckle. We all know where the turnbuckle is. It wasn't a head shot like a lot of head shots we see, but I do feel he targeted my head into the turnbuckle."

Fans in Montreal were also outraged by the lack of a suspension for Chára, and Quebec's director of criminal prosecutions, Louis Dionne, went so far as to request a criminal investigation. Even Pacioretty thought that was a bit much.

"I was disappointed that the NHL did not suspend Zdeno Chára," Pacioretty said in a statement. "However, I have no desire for him to be prosecuted legally. I feel that the incident, as ugly as it was, was part of a hockey game."

It wasn't until August that Montreal police announced they had closed the case, and that there would be no charges.

Sixteen days after Chára's hit on Pacioretty, the Canadiens visited Boston, and Chára had three assists in a 7–0 Bruins victory. Three nights later, Brad Marchand scored his 20th goal of the season on a power play to lift the Bruins to a 2–1 victory over the Flyers, clinching a playoff spot for the Bruins. The Bruins followed that with a 3–0 win over the Chicago Blackhawks in which Thomas recorded his ninth shutout of the year, and 42-year-old Mark Recchi moved into 12th place on the NHL's career scoring list with an assist that gave him 1,532 points. **Recchi had no interest, however, in → sticking around long enough to catch Ray Bourque, who was next on the list with 1,579 points.**

> Boston Bruins center Patrice Bergeron (37) hugs left wing Mark Recchi (28) after Recchi's assist on a Boston goal against the Chicago Blackhawks in the second period of an NHL hockey game in Boston on Tuesday, March 29, 2011. The Bruins won 3–0. AP PHOTO/ELISE AMENDOLA

> In this photo taken with a fisheye lens, Boston Bruins goalie Tim Thomas, foreground, looks behind as a shot by Montreal Canadiens' Mathieu Darche, right, goes in for a goal during the first period in Game 2 of a first-round NHL Stanley Cup playoffs hockey series in Boston, Saturday, April 16, 2011. AP PHOTO/WINSLOW TOWNSON

"I'm hoping we get on a long run," Recchi said. "It'll be real easy for me. If we win a championship, I'm gone."

The Bruins finished the regular season with a 46-25-11 record. Tim Thomas went 35-11-9, and set an NHL record with a save percentage of .938. Milan Lucic and David Krejčí led the team with 62 points each. Lucic scored his 30th goal of the season with 10 games remaining, but didn't score again. Bergeron and Horton joined Marchand as the Bruins' other 20-goal scorers. And the Bruins' 103 points were enough to win the Northeast Division and make them the three seed in the Eastern Conference. As fate would have it, the Canadiens were the six seed, setting up a first-round matchup for the two longtime rivals. It was the 33rd playoff matchup between the Bruins and Canadiens with Montreal winning 24 of the first 32.

The series opened with two games at TD Garden, and the Bruins lost them both. They were shutout 2–0 in the opener with Montreal's Brian Gionta scoring both goals, and then Chára was scratched for Game 2 due to dehydration, and the Bruins lost, 3-1. **The Bruins had lost the first two games of a playoff series for the 27th time in franchise history, and they were 0-26 in the previous series where it happened.**

> Boston Bruins' Michael Ryder (73) scores on Montreal Canadiens goaltender Carey Price during overtime of Game 4 of a first-round NHL Stanley Cup playoff series against the Montreal Canadiens in Montreal, Thursday, April 21, 2011.
AP PHOTO/THE CANADIAN PRESS, GRAHAM HUGHES

The Bruins rebounded by winning the next two games at the Bell Centre in Montreal. Krejčí, Horton, and Peverley scored the first three goals of Game 3, and after Tim Thomas let two soft goals go between his pads, Chris Kelly put in an empty netter in the game's final minute and the Bruins escaped with a 4–2 win. The Bruins fell behind 3–1 in Game 4, but goals by Andrew Ference and Bergeron tied it up. They fell behind again, but Kelly netted his second goal of the playoffs midway through the third period and the game went to overtime. Two minutes into overtime, the Bruins got a 3-on-1 break. Peverley's shot missed, but Kelly grabbed the puck behind the net, and **fed Michael Ryder, who settled the puck and then flipped it over a sprawling Carey Price.** It was Ryder's second goal of the game, and it evened the series at two games apiece.

A home team finally won a game when the Bruins took the fifth, 2–1, in double overtime. Just over nine minutes into the second extra session, Nathan Horton scooped up a rebound

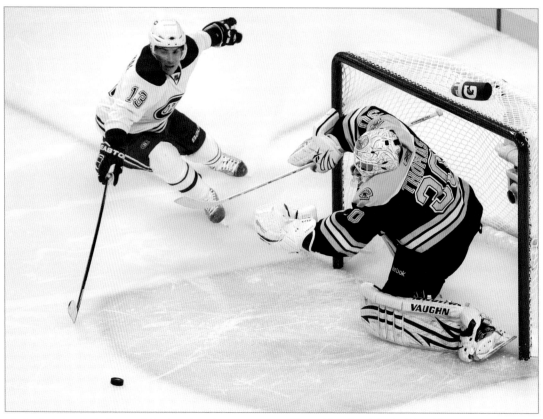

> Boston Bruins' goalie Tim Thomas, right, clears the puck away on a save as Montreal Canadiens left wing Michael Cammalleri, left, tries to gain possession during the second period in Game 5 of a first-round NHL Stanley Cup hockey playoff series in Boston, Saturday, April 23, 2011. AP PHOTO/CHARLES KRUPA

on the right side of the net and beat Price with the game winner. Price had stopped 49 shots. Thomas had 44 saves, and the biggest came three and a half minutes earlier when **he slid across the crease to stone Brian Gionta, who was looking at an open net from five feet away.**

The series moved back to Montreal, where the Canadiens scored a pair of 5-on-3 goals to beat the Bruins, 2–1, and force a seventh game. The Bruins played more than half of Game 6 without Lucic, who drove Jaroslav Špaček's head into the glass early in the second period. Lucic was given a boarding major and a game misconduct, and 16 seconds later, Bergeron was penalized for delay of game, and Gionta scored what proved to be the game winner on the ensuing two-man advantage.

So, there would be a Game 7 in Boston, and **Nathan Horton would score his second overtime goal of the series lifting the Bruins to a 4–3 win**, and

> Boston Bruins right wing Nathan Norton (18) beats Montreal Canadiens goalie Carey Price for the game-winning goal during the second overtime period in Game 5 of a first-round NHL Stanley Cup hockey playoff series in Boston, Saturday, April 23, 2011. The Bruins won 3–2, taking a 3-2 lead in the series. AP PHOTO/CHARLES KRUPA

a 4–3 series win. The Bruins jumped out to a 2–0 lead, but when Tomáš Plekanec stole the puck at center ice during a Bruins power play, he broke in on Thomas and scored, tying the game 2–2. The Bruins' power play was just awful during the series. They went 0-for-21 and were the first team to ever win a series without a power play goal. Kelly gave the Bruins a 3–2 lead with 10 minutes to go, but Bergeron was called for high sticking with 2:37 left and Montreal's P. K. Subban scored 30 seconds into the power play. That pushed the game to overtime where Lucic made a soft pass to a backward-skating Horton who slapped one home from the top of the crease, giving the Bruins their third overtime victory of the series, and sending them into the second round where they'd face the Flyers. Yes, there were a few more demons to exorcise!

There was certainly a lot of talk among Bruins and Flyers fans leading into the series about what happened the previous year, and that chatter only intensified when the Bruins once again won the first three games. They won Game 1 at the Wells Fargo Center in Philadelphia, 7–3,

A Star Player

"He was by far the star of the game," Bruins head coach Claude Julien said. "He stood tall, and if it wasn't for Timmy, we wouldn't be standing here with a win.**"**

> Boston Bruins' David Krejci, right, looks at his game-winning goal in the net past Philadelphia Flyers goalie Brian Boucher in the overtime period in Game 2 of the Eastern Conference semifinal NHL Stanley Cup playoffs series, Monday, May 2, 2011, in Philadelphia. The Bruins won 3–2. AP PHOTO/TOM MIHALEK

behind two goals each from Krejčí and Marchand. In the second game, the Flyers went up 2–0 before Thomas stopped the next 46 shots, and the Bruins came back to win it, 3–2, in overtime. **Krejčí got the game winner 14 minutes into overtime**, but Thomas was outstanding!

In Boston for Game 3, Chára and Krejčí scored in the opening 63 seconds and the Bruins went on to win, 5–1. So, for the second straight year they had a 3–0 lead on the Flyers. The Bruins made sure they didn't have a repeat of their collapse by sweeping the Flyers out of the playoffs in four straight. The Bruins broke open a 1–1 game with four unanswered goals in the third period. Lucic scored twice, and **Johnny Boychuk's 50-foot slapshot proved to be the game winner.** The Bruins got some good fortune when the top-seeded Washington Capitals were swept by the fifth-seeded Lightning. That meant the Bruins, who were going to the conference finals for the first time since 1992, would have home ice advantage.

> Boston Bruins defenseman Johnny Boychuk (55) celebrates his goal against the Philadelphia Flyers during the third period of Game 4 in a second-round NHL Stanley Cup hockey playoff series in Boston on Friday, May 6, 2011. AP PHOTO/ELISE AMENDOLA

Because the Bruins and Lightning had each won their respective series in four games, there was a lengthy delay before the start of the Eastern Conference Finals. By the time the puck dropped for Game 1, the Bruins hadn't played in eight days, and the Lightning had been off for 10. The rest appeared to do more good for Tampa Bay than the Bruins. The Lightning scored three goals in a span of 1:25 in the first period, and took Game 1, 5–2. It was their eighth straight victory.

The Bruins had to play the game without Patrice Bergeron, who, even with the extra time, still hadn't recovered from a concussion he suffered when he was hit by Claude Giroux in the third period of Game 7 against the Flyers. In his absence, Tyler Seguin saw his first playoff action. After playing in 76 regular-season games, Seguin was benched for the first 11 games of the playoffs. In his first action in over a month, Seguin had a goal and an assist. Then, with Bergeron still unable to play in Game 2, Seguin added two more goals and two more assists. Michael

Ryder also scored a pair of goals late in the second period that gave the Bruins a 6–3 lead, and the Bruins managed to hold on from there for a 6–5 win.

Game 3 was in Tampa, and Tim Thomas stopped all 31 shots he faced. He got the shutout while Ference and Krejčí got the goals, and the Bruins won 2–0. Krejčí's goal gave him six goals and 11 points in his last seven games.

Bergeron had returned for Game 3, and he scored twice in the first period of Game 4. The second goal came short-handed when he stole a pass from Lightning center Steven Stamkos and then scored on a slapshot from the top of the left faceoff circle. That gave the Bruins a 3–0 lead, but then they surrendered five unanswered goals, and lost 5–3.

The series was tied 2–2 and back in Boston for Game 5. In the second period, Horton scored his seventh goal of the playoffs, and Marchand added

> Boston Bruins goalie Tim Thomas, left, celebrates with teammate Nathan Horton (18) after they defeated the Tampa Bay Lightning in Game 7 of an NHL hockey Stanley Cup playoffs Eastern Conference final series, Friday, May 27, 2011, in Boston. The Bruins won 1–0 on Horton's goal in the third period. AP PHOTO/ELISE AMENDOLA

his sixth. The Bruins led 2–1 midway through the third period when Thomas made the save of the year! Eric Brewer shot from the point and the puck bounced off the boards right to Steve Downie. The net was wide open! But Thomas dove across the crease and reached out with his stick. Downie's shot caught the bottom edge of Thomas's stick. The one-goal lead was secured. The Bruins would add an empty netter later and won Game 5, 3–1.

"It was just reaction and, you know, desperation," Thomas said about the save on Downie. "I'll admit I got a little bit lucky there."

Tampa Bay's Teddy Purcell scored 36 seconds into Game 6, and despite Krejčí recording the Bruins' first playoff hat trick since Cam Neely did it in 1991, the Lightning evened the series with a 5–4 win. The Bruins were headed to their second Game 7 of these playoffs, and the game would be at the TD Garden on May 27, the latest date the Bruins had ever played.

Nathan Horton, who had the overtime game winner in Game 7 against Montreal, scored the only goal of Game 7 against Tampa Bay. With 7:33 to play, Krejčí skated toward the goal and slipped a pass over to Horton, who shot the puck inside the left post. Tim Thomas did the rest, stopping 24 shots, and the Bruins won, 1–0, earning their first trip to the Stanley Cup Finals since 1990. Their opponent would be the Vancouver Canucks, winners of the President's Trophy awarded to the team with the best regular-season record.

Game 1 at the Rogers Arena in Vancouver was scoreless for nearly a full 60 minutes, but with 18 seconds remaining, Ryan Kesler brought the puck into the Boston zone barely onsides and rifled a pass across the ice to Jannik Hansen. Chára dropped to the ice to block Hansen's shot, but Hansen threaded a pass to Raffi Torres, who was driving toward the net. Torres beat Thomas and the Canucks stunned the Bruins with a late goal. The Bruins lost Game 1, 1–0. **The game also featured Canucks forward Alex Burrows biting Patrice Bergeron!** It happened after the first period buzzer sounded and a scrum developed behind the Bruins net. Bergeron put his glove in Burrows's face and Burrows clearly chomped down on Bergeron's finger. It's the kind of thing that usually gets a player suspended, but the league issued a statement that it could not find any conclusive evidence that Burrows intentionally bit Bergeron's finger. All they had to do was look at the video. He did it!

But Burrows was not suspended for Game 2, and he proved to be the difference maker. He scored a power play goal in the first period,

> Vancouver Canucks left wing Alex Burrows, left, skirmishes with Boston Bruins center Patrice Bergeron after the first period of Game 1 of the Stanley Cup finals in Vancouver, Wednesday, June 1, 2011.
AP PHOTO/THE CANADIAN PRESS, JONATHAN HAYWARD

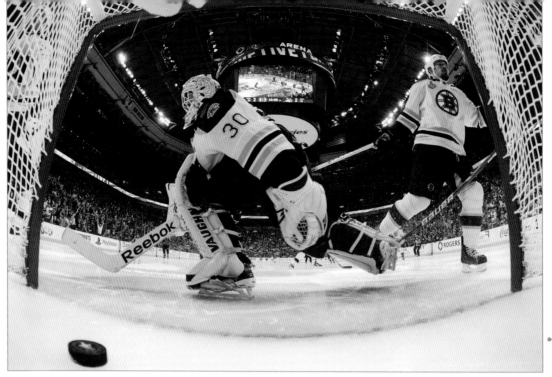

> Vancouver Canucks' Alex Burrows's game-winning goal goes past Boston Bruins goaltender Tim Thomas, left, as Bruins Andrew Ference looks on the first overtime period of Game 2 of the NHL hockey Stanley Cup Finals on Saturday, June 4, 2011, in Vancouver, British Columbia. AP PHOTO/BRUCE BENNETT, POOL

and after the Bruins took the lead on goals by Lucic and Recchi, Burrows assisted on the tying goal midway through the third period. The game went to overtime tied 2–2, and **Burrows ended it with a spectacular goal just 11 seconds into overtime.** Burrows went in on a breakaway, faked a slapshot that drew Thomas out of the net, and then beat Zdeno Chára around the back of the net and tucked the puck in for the game winner.

Vancouver led the series 2–0, and apparently felt empowered to mock the Bruins about the biting incident. During the third period of Game 2, Vancouver's Maxim Lapierre tried to stick his fingers in Bergeron's mouth, clearly taunting Bergeron, who didn't bite—literally or figuratively.

The series moved to Boston for Game 3, and it was the final game Nathan Horton would play: 5:04 into the first period, Horton skated into the Vancouver zone, and **the Canucks' Aaron Rome delivered a late, blind-side check with his shoulder right into Horton's jaw.** Horton suffered a severe concussion and left the ice on a stretcher and in a neck brace. Horton had eight goals and nine assists in the 20 playoff games to that point, and had a pair of Game 7 game-winning goals, but he was now lost for the rest of the series. Rome was given a five-minute major penalty for interference and a game misconduct. He would also receive a four-game suspension, which effectively ended his season as well.

> In this Monday, June 6, 2011, photo, Vancouver Canucks defenseman Aaron Rome (29) skates by as medical personnel tend to Boston Bruins right wing Nathan Horton, after Rome put a late hit on Horton in the first period during Game 3 of the NHL hockey Stanley Cup Finals in Boston. AP PHOTO/CHARLES KRUPA

The Bruins responded to the hit with an eight-goal eruption. Andrew Ference got it started 11 seconds into the second period. Recchi, Marchand (shorthanded), and Krejčí followed as the Bruins took a 4–0 lead to the third period. In the end, the Bruins took Game 3, 8–1, but they lost one of their most productive players.

"We talked a lot about playing for Horty," said Recchi, who scored twice. "It's tough to see your teammate down on the ice. We knew it was a late hit, but we're a little more concerned with his health at this point."

There were more incidents of taunting in Game 3 as well with Recchi and Lucic sticking their fingers in the faces of Burrows and Lapierre. So, after the game the league announced that any taunting moving forward would result in a two-minute penalty and a 10-minute game misconduct. That put an end to the silliness.

The Bruins remained inspired by Horton and continued to play well at home, winning Game 4 behind Tim Thomas's third shutout of the playoffs. Rich Peverley was moved up to the top line to replace Horton, and he scored twice. Ryder and Marchand scored the other goals and the Bruins won, 4–0.

Game 5 was back in Vancouver and for the second time in the series, Canucks goaltender Roberto Luongo shutout the Bruins. The only goal of the game was scored five minutes into the third period when Vancouver's Kevin Bieksa shot wide, and the puck bounced off the back boards right to Lapierre. Thomas had moved toward Bieksa's shot, and couldn't get back to

> Boston Bruins goalie Tim Thomas hoists the cup with the help of teammate Patrice Bergeron following the Bruins' 4–0 win over the Vancouver Canucks in Game 7 of the NHL hockey Stanley Cup Finals on Wednesday, June 15, 2011, in Vancouver, British Columbia. AP PHOTO/ THE CANADIAN PRESS, JONATHAN HAYWARD

cover the net in time before Lapierre shoveled the puck home. The Bruins went on to lose, 1–0, and before Game 6 back in Boston, Luongo made a comment that seemed to be critical of Thomas, and later tried to explain what he meant.

"I said also that he might make some saves that I don't," Luongo said. "So, I was just saying on that particular play, I would have played it different, and that's the difference between me and him. I've been pumping his tires ever since the series started, and I haven't heard one nice thing he had to say about me."

Told about Luongo's comments, Thomas got a laugh when he responded: "I guess I didn't realize it was my job to pump his tires. I guess I have to apologize for that."

Now, to this point in the series, Vancouver's league-leading goal-scoring offense had been held to six goals in five games. Former league MVP Henrik Sedin didn't have a point. NHL scoring champion Daniel Sedin had just one goal, and Vancouver's power play was 1-for-25. Yet, the Bruins trailed the series, 3–2.

Taking It One Game at a Time

Mark Recchi finished his career fifth on the all-time list for games played with 1,652.

Luongo didn't last past the 8:35 mark of the first period in Game 6. Marchand, Lucic, and Ference all put pucks past him in the game's opening minutes, and Luongo was pulled from the game. The Bruins won easily, 5–2.

Game 7 would be in Vancouver, and it would be the Bruins' 25th playoff game, all started by Tim Thomas. If the 37-year-old netminder was mentally or physically weary, it didn't show. **Thomas closed out an epic playoff performance with a 4–0 shutout.** He stopped all 37 shots he saw,

> Boston Bruins goalie Tim Thomas turns the puck away against the Vancouver Canucks during the third period of Game 7 of the NHL hockey Stanley Cup Finals on Wednesday, June 15, 2011, in Vancouver, British Columbia. AP PHOTO/THE CANADIAN PRESS, DARRYL DYCK

and the Bruins raised the Stanley Cup for the first time in 39 years. Bergeron and Marchand each scored twice, and Horton made his contribution by spraying a Gatorade bottle of water he brought with him from Boston on to the Rogers Arena ice 90 minutes before the opening faceoff.

"We wanted to put our ice on their ice and make it our ice," Horton explained.

It worked. And Tim Thomas would receive the Conn Smythe Trophy that goes to the Finals MVP. He stopped 238 of the 246 shots Vancouver put on net in the series. Later, he'd be awarded the Vezina Trophy as the top goaltender during the regular season, making him the first goalie to win the Stanley Cup along with the Conn Smythe and Vezina trophies in the same year since Bernie Parent did it for the Flyers in 1975.

"If I was going to do it any way, it would have to be the hardest way possible," Thomas said with a smile. "Three Game 7s in the playoffs, and to have to win it on the road in the final."

That's precisely how the Bruins won their sixth Stanley Cup, and New England's seventh championship trophy in nine years!

CHAPTER EIGHT

THE

2013 BOSTON RED SOX

Principal Owner:
John Henry

General Manager:
Ben Cherington

Manager:
John Farrell

Regular Season Record:
97-65

Regular Season Finish:
AL East Champions

Playoff Results:
Wild Card Round—Boston Red Sox defeated
Tampa Bay Rays (3–1)

Divisional Round—Boston Red Sox defeated
Detroit Tigers (4–2)

World Series:
Boston Red Sox defeated
St. Louis Cardinals (4–2)

Awards:
World Series MVP: DH David Ortiz

All-Stars: DH David Ortiz, 2B Dustin Pedroia

After winning the World Series in 2007, the Red Sox were once again a team trending in the wrong direction. They got as far as the American League Championship Series in 2008, but were knocked out of the divisional round in 2009, and then didn't even make the playoffs the next three years. They finished their 2011 season by losing 20 of their final 27 games and missing the playoffs for a second straight year. Some players later admitted to drinking beer and ordering Popeye's chicken during games. After eight years and two World Series titles, manager Terry Francona was fired. General manager Theo Epstein resigned. And then things got worse.

The 2012 season was marked by the debacle that was manager Bobby Valentine. He led the Red Sox to their lowest win total in a full season in 46 years. At 69-93, the Red Sox finished last in their division, and Valentine was fired the day after the season ended.

Rebuilding the Red Sox into a championship contender began on October 21 with the hiring of John Farrell as the new manager. Farrell had been the Red Sox pitching coach from 2007 to 2010, and left to become manager of the Toronto Blue Jays.

Red Sox general manager Ben Cherington spent the rest of the offseason adding important veterans who provided stability and leadership in the clubhouse and were productive on the field. When the acquisition frenzy concluded, the revamped Red Sox roster included catcher David Ross, outfielders Jonny Gomes and Shane Victorino, first basemen Mike Napoli and Mike Carp, 35-year-old starting pitcher Ryan Dempster, relief pitcher Koji Uehara, and shortstop Stephen Drew. All of those players were signed as free agents, and in a trade with the Pittsburgh Pirates the Red Sox also acquired closer Joel Hanrahan and utility player Brock Holt. Twenty-two-year-old outfielder Jackie Bradley Jr. also earned a spot in the Opening Day lineup by hitting .419 in spring training.

The Red Sox opened the 2013 season by winning two out of three in New York and again in Toronto. By the time they got home, Jon Lester had won twice, and third baseman Will Middle-brooks had four home runs. He hit three of them on the final day of the road trip. Also, John Lackey was placed on the 15-day disabled list with a right biceps strain.

Daniel Nava's three-run homer in the seventh lifted Clay Buchholz and the Red Sox to a 3–1 victory over Baltimore in their home opener, but the Red Sox dropped their next two games. They were 7-4 on the morning of Monday, April 15, 2013. It was the annual Patriots Day game played while thousands ran the Boston Marathon and many more thousands lined the streets of Boston to cheer the runners along the route.

At about 2:10 in → **the afternoon, Mike Napoli doubled to left-center field to score Dustin Pedroia** with the game-winning run in the ninth inning. The Red

> Boston Red Sox' Mike Napoli is mobbed by teammates after his game-winning double scored teammate Dustin Pedroia during the ninth inning of Boston's 3–2 win over the Tampa Bay Rays in a baseball game at Fenway Park in Boston on Monday, April 15, 2013.
AP PHOTO/WINSLOW TOWNSON

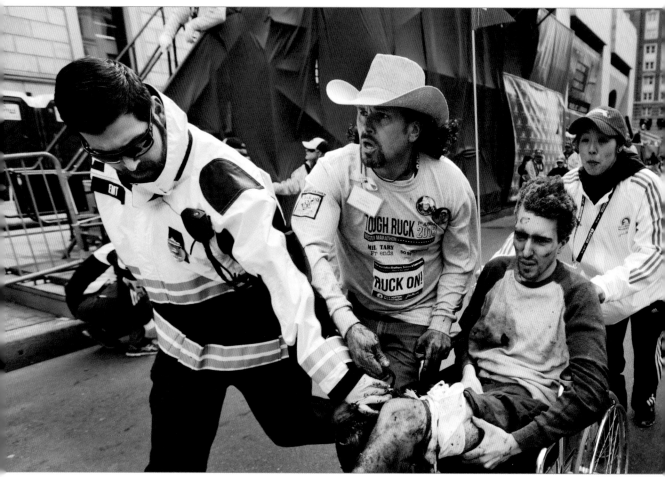

> In this Monday, April 15, 2013, file photo, an emergency responder and volunteers, including Carlos Arredondo, center in cowboy hat, push Jeff Bauman in a wheelchair after he was injured in one of two explosions near the finish line of the Boston Marathon. On Friday, May 15, 2015, Dzhokhar Tsarnaev was sentenced to death by lethal injection for the terror attack. AP PHOTO/CHARLES KRUPA

Sox celebrated a walkoff 3–2 victory over the Rays. About 40 minutes later, and one mile away, two pressure cooker bombs exploded in Copley Square, killing three people and injuring at least 264 others. **The Red Sox were unaware of the terrorist act as they left the ballpark and boarded a plane for Cleveland, but they soon found out.**

"I got very angry," David Ortiz, recovering in Pawtucket from an Achilles tendon injury, told the *Providence Journal*. "Why people would do things like that, man? Watching the news last night, I saw this 8-year-old kid that was right there with his mom and his sister, waiting for his dad to cross the finish line. All I think about, man, is how this could happen?"

The Boston Marathon bombing was a horrible tragedy exacting physical and emotional pain on countless victims, and it also united a city and all of New England. Within hours of the explosion, the hashtag #BostonStrong trended on Twitter. The next day, emotional Red Sox players talked about being part of the community, and having walked the street with their families just days earlier right where the bombs exploded. Will Middlebrooks wrote "Boston Strong" on his cleats, and at the suggestion of Jonny Gomes, the Red Sox created a jersey with the area code for Boston, 617, in between the words "Boston Strong."

"It was just something to let them know they're out of sight right now, but definitely not out of mind," Gomes said. "We just wanted to let people know we've got a heavy heart over here."

The jersey hung in the dugout each day as the Red Sox went out and swept a three-game series from the Indians. The Red Sox had stretched their winning streak to six games, and were headed home for their first game at Fenway Park since the Marathon Bombing, but that game would have to wait. In the early morning hours of April 19, one of the bombers, Tamerlan Tsarnaev, was killed in an encounter with Watertown police. The city of Boston was put on lockdown while law enforcement hunted down the other bomber, Dzhokhar Tsarnaev. So, the 7:00 p.m. scheduled game against the Kansas City Royals was postponed. At approximately 8:15 that night, Dzhokhar Tsarnaev was discovered hiding in a boat in the backyard of a Watertown home. He was captured, and a city could breathe a sigh of relief. The Red Sox played the following day. Before the game, a special ceremony was held to honor the victims and law enforcement. David Ortiz, coming off the disabled list to play in his first game of the season, walked to the pitcher's mound, and wearing a white home jersey with "Boston" on the front, addressed the crowd.

The Quarter-Billions-Dollar Trade

On August 25, 2012, the Red Sox sent Adrian Gonzalez, Carl Crawford and Josh Beckett to the Los Angeles Dodgers in a nine-player trade. It was a $250 million salary dump that allowed the Red Sox to rebuild.

> A young fan holds a "Boston Strong" sign before a baseball game between the Boston Red Sox and the Kansas City Royals in Boston, Saturday, April 20, 2013. AP PHOTO/MICHAEL DWYER

"This jersey that we wear today, it doesn't say Red Sox," Ortiz began. "It says Boston. We want to thank you Mayor Menino, Governor Patrick, the whole police department for the great job that they did this past week. This is our fucking city! And nobody gonna dictate our freedom. Stay strong!"

Recording artist Neil Diamond made a surprise appearance and sang a live version of his hit "Sweet Caroline" before the bottom of the eighth inning, and then Daniel Nava blasted a three-run homer into the right field bullpen. The Red Sox won their seventh game in a row, 4–3.

The Red Sox played the entire season with a sympathetic understanding and an open heart for the people of New England. The team recognized and accepted its role as a unifying, therapeutic, and hopeful force. And they weren't burdened by it. They were carried by it! Boston Strong was a two-way street. The Red Sox gained strength as they were giving it.

However, the spirit and magic of the season would have to wait a day. The Red Sox and Royals made up the game postponed by the city's lockdown by playing a day-night doubleheader

▸ A Boston Red Sox' David Ortiz pumps his fist in front of an American flag and a line of Boston Marathon volunteers, background, after addressing the crowd before a baseball game between the Boston Red Sox and the Kansas City Royals in Boston, Saturday, April 20, 2013. AP PHOTO/MICHAEL DWYER

on Sunday, April 21. In the first game, Jonny Gomes went to the plate with the names of the four people killed in the Marathon attack and the ensuing manhunt imprinted on his bat. The Red Sox lost both games that day, but they won the following day when the Red Sox honored the Watertown, Massachusetts, police officers who helped kill one of the bombers and capture the other.

The Red Sox put together another five-game winning streak and finished April with a franchise-tying record 18 wins. Ortiz was phenomenal! In his first nine games coming off the disabled list, he batted .500 with three homers and 15 RBIs. But the good times that never felt so good didn't last. The Red Sox lost nine of 11 games in early May, and began the month losing 12 of 22 games. It would have been worse if not for some last-inning heroics along the way. The Red Sox won twice in extra innings, and on May 16, Will Middlebrooks hit a two-strike, two-out, three-run double in the ninth inning to beat the Tampa Bay Rays, 4–3. The victory was part of a five-game winning streak in which the Red Sox appeared to have righted the ship.

In June, the Red Sox began by taking a couple of games from the Yankees. Clay Buchholz improved to 8-0 with a rain-shortened shutout in New York, and two days later, David Ortiz hit

> Boston Red Sox' Clay Buchholz pitches in the first inning of the second game of a baseball doubleheader against the Los Angeles Angels in Boston, Saturday, June 8, 2013. AP PHOTO/MICHAEL DWYER

his 11th career walkoff home run to beat the Texas Rangers, 6–3. On June 8, Buchholz won again, but left the game against the Angels with neck stiffness. **He was 9-0 with a 1.71 ERA to that point in the season, but he wouldn't pitch again until September 10.** Even without Buchholz, the Red Sox finished the month strong. On the final day of June, the Red Sox celebrated another walkoff victory when Shane Victorino's groundball to first was misplayed and Jonathan Diaz raced home with the winning run. The 5–4 victory gave the Red Sox a 50-34 record, best in the American League. It was just the fourth time in team history that the Red Sox had 50 wins by the end of June.

The Red Sox began July by sweeping the San Diego Padres in three straight at Fenway Park, and then beginning a 10-game West Coast road trip with a 6–2 win at Anaheim. In taking three out of four from the Seattle Mariners, the Red Sox rallied back from four-run deficits twice, and **Ortiz set the record for most hits by a designated hitter**. His double to left-center field off the Mariners' Aaron Harang on July 10 was his 1,689th hit as a DH, breaking

> Boston Red Sox' David Ortiz responds to the cheers of fans after he hit a double in the second inning of a baseball game against the Seattle Mariners, Wednesday, July 10, 2013, in Seattle. With the hit, Ortiz's 1,689th in his MLB career, he passed the record held by Harold Baines for the most hits as a designated hitter in major league history. AP PHOTO/TED S. WARREN

the record established by Harold Baines. Despite losing the final game of the first half in 11 innings to the Blue Jays, the Red Sox cruised into the All-Star break with a major-league best 58-39 record.

The second half of the season began at Fenway Park, where the Red Sox took two of three from the Yankees. **In the series finale, Mike Napoli's second home run of the game was a walkoff blast** into the center field bleachers. The Red Sox won 8–7 in 11 innings, but when they lost three of the next four games, they also lost the grip they had for two months on first place in the East. Suddenly, they were chasing the Tampa Bay Rays. Perhaps that's what prompted them to make a move before the trading deadline. In a three-team, seven-player deal with the White Sox and Tigers, the Red Sox

> Boston Red Sox' Mike Napoli, center left, celebrates his walk-off home run in the eleventh inning of a baseball game against the New York Yankees in Boston, Monday, July 22, 2013. The Red Sox won 8–7. AP PHOTO/MICHAEL DWYER

> Boston Red Sox' Daniel Nava, right, celebrates his RBI single that drove in the winning run in the ninth inning of a baseball game against the Seattle Mariners in Boston, Thursday, Aug. 1, 2013. The Red Sox won 8–7. AP PHOTO/MICHAEL DWYER

gave up their young shortstop Jose Iglesias, but bolstered their starting rotation with veteran right-hander Jake Peavy. Before Peavy arrived, the Red Sox re-took the division lead when they battled the Seattle Mariners for 15 innings on the final day of July.

In that game, Gomes ended the top of the 15th inning with an unassisted double play, a rare achievement for an outfielder. With runners on first and second, Gomes charged in from his left field position, and made a diving catch. Instead of lobbing the ball to second base to double off the runner, Gomes got up and ran the ball in, touching second base for the unassisted double play. Stephen Drew ended the game in the bottom half of the inning with a bases-loaded single.

The next day, the Red Sox stunned the Mariners with a six-run rally in the ninth inning. Trailing 7–2, **Daniel Nava started the inning with a walk, and ended it with a bases-loaded single to complete the comeback.** The Red Sox won, 8–7.

"In a word," John Farrell said, "magical!"

Peavy, the 2007 National League Cy Young Award winner, made his Red Sox debut two days later, and the Red Sox beat the Arizona Diamondbacks, 5–2. Then the magic continued in a crazy

> Boston Red Sox' Stephen Drew hits a three-run homer to go ahead of the Houston Astros in the ninth inning of a baseball game Wednesday, Aug. 7, 2013, in Houston. Boston won 7–5. AP PHOTO/PAT SULLIVAN

game against the Houston Astros. Knuckleballer Steven Wright made his first big-league start for the Red Sox, and catcher Ryan Lavarnway had a little trouble handling the knuckleball. He had four passed balls in the first inning and the Red Sox fell behind 5–0, but Jacoby Ellsbury homered twice and Gomes hit a three-run homer to help the Red Sox rally back for a 15–10 win. It was Boston's 69th win, which matched their win total from the previous year, and there were still 47 games left in the season. **The next night, Stephen Drew smashed a three-run homer in the ninth inning to beat the Astros, 7–5.** And the "cardiac kids" did it again on August 13th when Shane Victorino hit a two-run single to beat the Blue Jays, 4–2, in 11 innings. That was the 19th time the Red Sox had won a game in their final at-bat. The next night, also against Toronto, Mike Napoli hit a game-tying, two-run homer with two outs in the ninth inning, but the Red Sox lost it in the 10th, 4–3. Even the losses were exciting!

The Red Sox won nine of the remaining 15 games in August, including another last at-bat victory against the Orioles, in which Mike Carp hit a soft single over third base in the eighth

> Boston Red Sox' Jarrod Saltalamacchia watches his grand slam in front of New York Yankees catcher Chris Stewart during the seventh inning of a baseball game at Fenway Park in Boston on Friday, Sept. 13, 2013. AP PHOTO/ELISE AMENDOLA

inning to score Jarrod Saltalamacchia. Koji Uehara pitched a perfect ninth for his 14th save of the year, and the Red Sox won, 4–3.

Wins were coming in bunches for the Red Sox. They won six of their last seven to close out August, and won six of their first seven to begin September. Along the way, Jon Lester outdueled Detroit's 19-game winner, Max Scherzer, and the Red Sox tied a franchise record with eight home runs en route to beating the Tigers, 20–4. The Red Sox followed that up with 34 runs in three games at Yankee Stadium. They twice scored runs in the ninth inning against Yankees closer Mariano Rivera, and narrowly missed making it a four-game sweep when the Yankees' Ichiro Suzuki scored on Brandon Workman's wild pitch with two outs in the ninth inning, and the Red Sox lost, 4–3.

Two nights later on September 10, Clay Buchholz made his first start since early June, giving up three hits in five shutout innings. He improved to 10-0, and lowered his ERA to 1.61. The next night, Mike Carp hit a pinch-hit grand slam in the 10th inning, and the Red Sox won again!

After a sweep of the Yankees at Fenway Park that included **a Jarrod Saltalamacchia grand slam,** the Red Sox were 92-59. They had won 17 of their last 21 games, and led the American League East by 9.5 games over Tampa Bay.

The Red Sox clinched a playoff spot with eight games remaining in the regular season. **John Lackey sealed the deal with a two-hit complete-game** 3–1 victory over the Orioles. The Red Sox didn't celebrate that night, but the following night, when they clinched the division title with a 6–3 win over the Toronto Blue Jays, they rushed from the dugout and danced on the pitcher's mound. Champagne was uncorked, and a beer-soaked celebration continued in the clubhouse.

There were still seven games left in the regular season, and the Red Sox only won three of them, but that was enough to finish with 97 wins and the best record in the American League. That was an incredible team accomplishment, because as individuals, the Red Sox did not have many players with career years. Their pitching staff finished with the 14th-best ERA in

Through It All

" To go through some of the things we've gone through the past three years," said Jon Lester, who got the game-clinching win and had posted a 2.29 ERA since the All-Star break, "the injuries and nonsense and everything, to finally be back at this point is very, very rewarding. **"**

> Boston Red Sox' John Lackey, left, gets the ball from Jonny Gomes after pitching nine innings and defeating the Baltimore Orioles 3–1 in a baseball game in Boston, Thursday, Sept. 19, 2013. AP PHOTO/MICHAEL DWYER

baseball. Their starting rotation was led by Jon Lester, who was a solid ace, but only went 15-8. John Lackey and Ryan Dempster both had losing records, and were a combined 18-22. Clay Buchholz finished 12-1, but only made 16 starts. And Jake Peavy and Felix Doubront both had ERAs over 4.00. The strength of the Red Sox remained their consistent and productive offense that led all of baseball in runs scored. David Ortiz and Mike Napoli set the pace by combining for 53 homers and 195 RBIs. But would the Red Sox be able to hit as well in the postseason as they did in the regular season?

The playoffs opened at Fenway Park on October 4 against the Tampa Bay Rays, and the Red Sox won the first two games by scoring 19 runs on 25 hits. In the opener, they trailed 2–0 in the fourth inning after Lester had given up solo home runs to the Rays' Sean Rodríguez and Ben Zobrist. Pedroia led off the fourth with a sharp single, and then the floodgates opened up. The Rays played some shoddy defense and the Red Sox scored five runs in the inning. When the game was over, every Red Sox player in the starting lineup had at least one hit and one run scored, something that hadn't been done in the postseason since the 1936 Yankees. It was a testament to the quality and the depth of the Red Sox lineup. The Red Sox won 12–2, and followed it up

> Boston Red Sox' David Ortiz hits a solo home run off Tampa Bay Rays starting pitcher David Price in front of Rays catcher Jose Molina during the first inning in Game 2 of baseball's American League division series, Saturday, Oct. 5, 2013, in Boston. AP PHOTO/STEPHAN SAVOIA

with a 7–4 win the next day. **David Ortiz enjoyed his first two-home-run game in the playoffs, hitting his blasts in the first and eighth innings off left-hander David Price.**

Game 3 in Tampa was an exciting one! Buchholz gave up a game-tying three-run homer to Evan Longoria in the fifth inning. That made it 3–3. The Rays went ahead with a run in the eighth, but the Red Sox tied it up in the ninth when Pedroia's grounder to short scored Bogaerts. So, they went to the bottom of the ninth inning tied 4–4. Koji Uehara, who hadn't given up a home run in his last 37 appearances going all the way back to June 30, and who had only given up one run in his last 40⅓ innings, gave up a walkoff home run to José Lobatón. With two outs in the bottom of the ninth inning, Lobatón drove the ball over the center field wall. The ball bounced off a fan's glove and landed in the 10,000-gallon fish tank where cownose rays swim. The Rays won, 5–4.

▸ Boston Red Sox' designated hitter David Ortiz celebrates his solo home run off Tampa Bay Rays starting pitcher David Price in the first inning in Game 2 of baseball's American League division series Saturday, Oct. 5, 2013, in Boston. AP PHOTO/CHARLES KRUPA

Uehara bounced back and got the final four outs of Game 4, and the Red Sox advanced to the American League Championship Series for the first time since 2008. Game 4 starter Jake Peavy pitched 5⅔ innings, allowing just one run. And the Red Sox scored their three runs on a wild pitch, an infield single, and a ninth-inning sacrifice fly off the bat of Pedroia. The Red Sox won the series clincher, 3–1, and would have four days off before welcoming the Detroit Tigers into Fenway Park for the start of the ALCS.

The Tigers were loaded! Their roster included a pair of aces in Max Scherzer, who went 21-3 and would win the Cy Young Award in 2013, and Justin Verlander, the Cy Young Award winner two years earlier; and slugger Miguel Cabrera, who would win the second of back-to-back MVP awards in 2013. The strength of the Tigers' pitching staff was evident in Game 1 when their third-best starter Aníbal Sánchez and four relievers combined in a one-hit shutout. The Tigers came within two outs of a no-hitter. Daniel Nava's clean single to center field with one out in the ninth was the only Red Sox hit of the game. The Red Sox struck out 17 times, and they lost 1–0.

"It was a great game," said Jon Lester, who gave up a sixth-inning RBI single to Jhonny Peralta for the game's only run. "That was playoff baseball."

The excitement, along with Detroit's pitching dominance, continued into Game 2. Scherzer didn't give up a base hit until Shane Victorino's two-out single in the sixth inning. By then the Red Sox were already down 5–0. Miguel Cabrera and Alex Avila had homered in the top of the sixth against Clay Buchholz, and it looked as though the Red Sox would drop the first two games of the series. And then David Ortiz happened!

Batting with the bases loaded in the eighth inning and the Red Sox trailing, 5–1, Ortiz sent the first pitch he saw against reliever Joaquin Benoit into the right field bullpen. A grand slam!

> Boston Red Sox' Jonny Gomes scores the winning run on a hit by Jarrod Saltalamacchia during Game 2 of the American League baseball championship series against the Detroit Tigers Sunday, Oct. 13, 2013, in Boston. At right is Detroit Tigers' Alex Avila.
AP PHOTO/MATT SLOCUM

Ortiz's first postseason grand slam tied the game 5–5. The Tigers then gifted the Red Sox the win when **Gomes led off the ninth with an infield single, moved to second on a throwing error, to third on a wild pitch, and scored on Saltalamacchia's single through a drawn in infield.** The Red Sox won 6–5 and went to Detroit with the series tied 1–1.

Game 3 was another 1–0 pitchers' duel, but this time the Red Sox prevailed. Mike Napoli's seventh-inning home run against Justin Verlander accounted for the game's only run. It was the first run scored against Verlander in 33 innings, and coincidentally, Napoli's very first at-bat in the big leagues was a home run against Verlander. For the Red Sox, it was all about John Lackey coming up huge! His time with the Red Sox had not gone well up to this point. After signing a five-year, $82.5 million contract, Lackey pitched poorly his first two seasons with the Red Sox. He missed his third season entirely after having elbow surgery, and returned for the 2013 season and went just 10-13. However, locked into a battle with Verlander, Lackey kept the Tigers off the scoreboard until he was pulled with two outs in the seventh. In the eighth, the Tigers put runners on first and third with one out, but Junichi Tazawa struck out Cabrera, and Koji Uehara did the same to Prince Fielder to end the threat. Uehara closed it out in the ninth. In three games, the Red Sox had struck out 35 times in 21 innings against Detroit's starters, but they still led the series, 2–1.

Detroit got another fine performance from their starter, Doug Fister, in Game 4. He gave up a run in six innings, while the Tigers pounded Jake Peavy for seven runs in three innings. The Tigers went on to even the series easily, 7–3. That set up a rematch of Game 1 starters Jon Lester and Aníbal Sánchez in a pivotal Game 5 at Comerica Park. This time, Lester came out on top.

Mike Napoli got the scoring started with a 460-foot home run to center field in the second inning. The Red Sox scored three times in the inning, and then added a crucial fourth run in the third inning when Napoli doubled, moved to third on a groundout, and scored on a two-out, two-strike wild pitch. That made the score 4–0, but proved to be the game-winning run, because the Tigers chipped away at the lead before finally falling, 4–3. The wild pitch was one example of the Tigers self-inflicting their own misery. Cabrera being thrown out at the plate by a mile in the first inning was another. Lester gave up two runs in 5⅔ innings, and the Red Sox were headed back to Boston with a chance to close out the series.

Game 6 was Shane Victorino's moment. The Red Sox came up to bat in the bottom of the seventh inning trailing, 2–1. Gomes hit a leadoff double and, after Stephen Drew struck out, Xander Bogaerts walked putting runners on first and second. Ball four to Bogaerts was pitch

> Boston Red Sox' Shane Victorino hits a grand slam against the Detroit Tigers in the seventh inning during Game 6 of the American League baseball championship series on Saturday, Oct. 19, 2013, in Boston. AP PHOTO/CHARLIE RIEDEL

number 110 for Max Scherzer, and he was pulled from the game. Jacoby Ellsbury followed with what was potentially a double-play ball that would have ended the inning, but Tigers shortstop Jose Iglesias booted the ball. That loaded the bases for Victorino.

Another pitching change brought José Veras to the hill. He threw three straight looping curveballs. The first two were strikes. **Victorino jumped on the third one** and knocked it into to the Monster seats in left. Another grand slam for the Red Sox!

The Red Sox bullpen did the rest—Uehara striking out Iglesias to end the game—and the Red Sox won, 5–2, and were back in the World Series for the third time in 10 years.

> Boston Red Sox starting pitcher Jon Lester throws during the first inning of Game 1 of baseball's World Series against the St. Louis Cardinals Wednesday, Oct. 23, 2013, in Boston. AP PHOTO/CHARLES KRUPA

As it was in 2004, the Red Sox opponent was the St. Louis Cardinals. **Game 1 should be remembered for Jon Lester's 7⅔ scoreless innings**, but it was the Cardinals' uncharacteristically sloppy play that drew most of the attention. In the first inning, David Ortiz hit what should have been an inning-ending double-play ball at second baseman Matt Carpenter. He flipped the ball to defensive specialist Pete Kozma, who dropped the ball. Second-base umpire Dana DeMuth initially called Dustin Pedroia out at second, but a conference of six umpires resulted in the call being overturned. The bases were loaded for Mike Napoli, and he roped a line drive to left-center giving the Red Sox a 3–0 lead.

In the second inning, Cardinal starter Adam Wainwright and catcher Yadier Molina let an easy popup by Stephen Drew fall between them, and Kozma made another error, leading to two more Red Sox runs. A David Ortiz two-run homer in the seventh would make it 7–0, and the Red Sox went on to win their ninth consecutive World Series game, 8–1.

Playoff Power

Ortiz hit 17 playoff home runs in his Red Sox career. Manny Ramirez holds the MLB record for playoff home runs with 29, but only hit 11 while with the Red Sox.

Ortiz hit another two-run homer in Game 2, this one in the sixth inning to give the Red Sox a 2–1 lead, but the Cardinals responded by chasing John Lackey in the seventh inning and taking a 4–2 lead. Neither team scored again, and the series moved to St. Louis tied one game apiece.

Game 3 provided one of the wildest and weirdest finishes to a World Series game ever! On the final play of the game, the Red Sox threw two Cardinal runners out at the plate, but the second one was called safe, because **third baseman Will Middlebrooks was called for interference.** Both teams rushed toward home plate—the Cardinals celebrating a walkoff victory, and the Red Sox racing out to find out what had happened.

> St. Louis Cardinals' Allen Craig gets tangled with Boston Red Sox' Will Middlebrooks during the ninth inning of Game 3 of baseball's World Series Saturday, Oct. 26, 2013, in St. Louis. Middlebrooks was called for obstruction on the play and Craig went in to score the game-winning run. The Cardinals won 5–4 to take a 2-1 lead in the series. AP PHOTO/DAVID J. PHILLIP

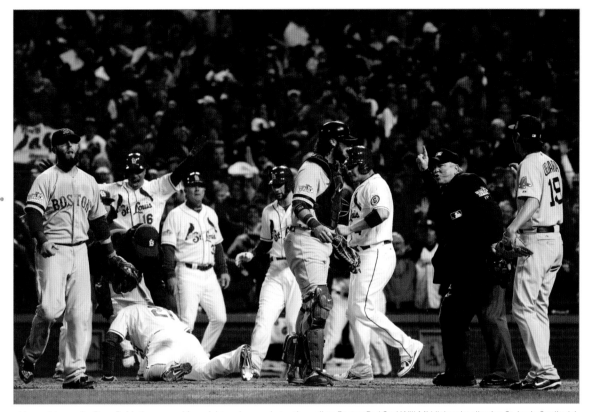

> Home plate umpire Dana DeMuthm, second from right, makes an obstruction call on Boston Red Sox' Will Middlebrooks allowing St. Louis Cardinals' Allen Craig, on ground, to score the game-winning run in the ninth inning of Game 3 of baseball's World Series Saturday, Oct. 26, 2013, in St. Louis. The Cardinals won 5–4 to take a 2-1 lead in the series. AP PHOTO/MATT SLOCUM

Here's what happened: A two-run single in the eighth inning by Xander Bogaerts tied the game 4–4. In the bottom of the ninth, the Cardinals put runners on second and third with one out. The Red Sox played their infield in, and the strategy appeared to work when John Jay grounded the ball to second. Pedroia made a great diving play to backhand the ball and threw a perfect strike home to get the lead runner. Red Sox catcher Jarrod Saltalamacchia tagged out Yadier Molina, and then threw to third base to try to get the slow-moving Allen Craig. Saltalamacchia's throw hit Craig as he slid into third base, and the ball deflected into foul territory in left field. Craig jumped up to race home, but he tripped over Red Sox third baseman Will Middlebrooks, who had fallen to his stomach trying to catch Saltalamacchia's throw. When Craig tripped, the third-base umpire immediately called Middlebrooks for interference. So, even though Daniel Nava tracked down the ball in left field and threw home in time to get Craig, the home-plate umpire called Craig safe. The interference call was correct, because it didn't matter if Middlebrooks

> Boston Red Sox first baseman Mike Napoli celebrates after tagging out St. Louis Cardinals' Kolten Wong on a pick-off attempt to end Game 4 of baseball's World Series Sunday, Oct. 27, 2013, in St. Louis. The Red Sox won 4–2 to tie the series at 2-2. AP PHOTO/DAVID J. PHILLIP

intended to interfere. The fact that he was on the ground in the basepath and Craig stumbled over him was enough for interference to be called. The Cardinals won Game 3, 5–4.

"Tough way to have a game end," Red Sox manager John Farrell said, "Particularly of this significance."

Game 4 ended when Red Sox closer **Koji Uehara picked off rookie pinch-runner Kolten Wong** with Carlos Beltran representing the tying run at the plate. Of the 1,404 postseason games in major-league history, there had never been a game that ended with either an obstruction call or a pickoff play, and then both occurred on back-to-back days. So, it was a crazy first four games of the World Series.

Game 4 also included a sixth-inning pep talk by David Ortiz, who brought the team around him in the dugout and said:

"Let's loosen up. Let's try to play baseball the way we normally do."

Jonny Gomes said later it was a powerful message that got everyone's attention. "It was like 24 kindergarteners looking up at their teacher," Gomes added. And then he went out and blasted

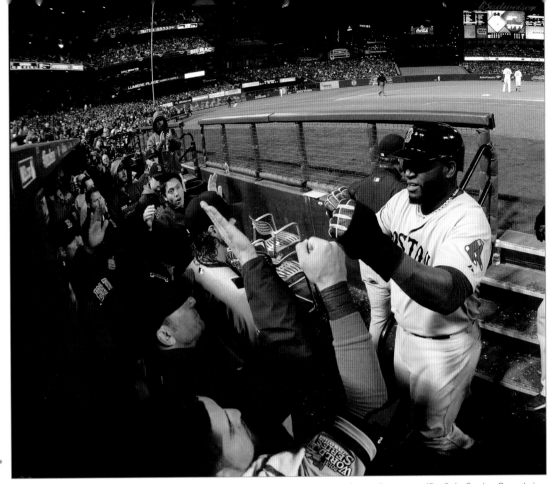

> Boston Red Sox designated hitter David Ortiz, right, is congratulated by his teammates after scoring on a sacrifice fly by Stephen Drew during the fifth inning of Game 4 of baseball's World Series against the St. Louis Cardinals Sunday, Oct. 27, 2013, in St. Louis.
AP PHOTO/MATT SLOCUM

a go-ahead three-run homer in the seventh inning. John Lackey, still scheduled to pitch Game 6, was called upon to give the Red Sox an inning in relief, and he pitched a perfect eighth inning. Uehara closed out the 4–2 victory, and the series was tied two games each.

Jon Lester was outstanding again in Game 5, and this time people took notice. He allowed one run and struck out seven in 7⅔ innings, and outpitched Adam Wainwright for a 3–1 victory. In three career World Series starts, Lester was now 3-0 with a 0.43 ERA.

David Ortiz had three more hits, including an RBI double in the first inning. To this point in the series, Ortiz was 11-for-15 with two home runs, six RBIs, and four walks.

"I was born for this," Ortiz said with a big smile!

David Ross had the big hit in Game 5, a ground-rule double in the seventh inning to give the Red Sox a 2–1 lead. Jacoby Ellsbury followed with an RBI groundout and the Red Sox went

> The Boston Red Sox celebrate after defeating the St. Louis Cardinals in Game 6 of baseball's World Series Wednesday, Oct. 30, 2013, in Boston. The Red Sox won 6–1 to win the series. AP PHOTO/DAVID J. PHILLIP

on to win, 3–1. They were headed home to Fenway Park needing just one more win for another World Series title.

In Game 6, the Red Sox faced the Cardinals, sensational 22-year-old rookie, Michael Wacha, who was 4-0 with a 1.00 ERA in his first postseason, but the Red Sox knocked him out of the game in the fourth inning. Shane Victorino, who had missed the previous two games with a bad back, returned to hit a three-run double off the Green Monster. And the slumping Stephen Drew led off the fourth with a home run into the right-center field bullpen. John Lackey pitched into the seventh inning to earn the series-clinching win, and the Red Sox went on to close it out in undramatic fashion, 6–1. **For the first time in 95 years, the Red Sox were able to celebrate a World Series title at home!**

When Koji Uehara struck out Matt Carpenter for the final out, the celebration began. The crowd cheered! The song "Dirty Water" blared over the loudspeakers, and players and their families danced on the field. Once again, as he had done when the Red Sox returned following

> Boston Red Sox' Jonny Gomes places the championship trophy and a Red Sox baseball jersey at the Boston Marathon Finish Line during a pause in their World Series victory rolling rally in Boston, Saturday, Nov. 2, 2013, to remember those affected by the Marathon bombing.
AP PHOTO/ELISE AMENDOLA

the Boston Marathon bombings, Ortiz stood on the field, microphone in hand, and addressed the city.

"This is for you, Boston," he said. "You guys deserve it. We've been through a lot this year, and this is for all of you and all those families who struggled."

The Cardinals had walked Ortiz four times in Game 6, including three times intentionally, so he finished the series with an other worldly .760 on-base percentage, second highest in World Series history. He was named the World Series MVP, and said this World Series victory "might be the most special" to him.

During the duck boat parade through Boston three days later, Jonny Gomes placed the World Series trophy and a Red Sox "Boston Strong" jersey at the finish line of the Boston Marathon. Classical singer Ronan Tynan led the crowd in an emotional rendition of "God Bless America." The Red Sox were World Series champions once again, but more importantly, Boston was strong again!

CHAPTER NINE

2014 NEW ENGLAND PATRIOTS

Owner:
Robert Kraft

Director of Player Personnel:
Nick Caserio

Head Coach:
Bill Belichick

Regular Season Record:
12-4

Regular Season Finish:
AFC East Champions

Playoff Results:
Divisional Round—New England Patriots 35
Baltimore Ravens 31

AFC Championship—New England Patriots 45
Indianapolis Colts 7

Super Bowl:
New England Patriots 28
Seattle Seahawks 24

Awards:
Super Bowl MVP: QB Tom Brady

Pro Bowlers: QB Tom Brady,
K Stephen Gostkowski, TE Rob Gronkowski,
CB Darrelle Revis, WR Matthew Slater

Heading into the 2014 season, the Patriots had gone nine years since their last Super Bowl win. In those nine years, they had won their division and gone to the playoffs eight times. They'd been to two Super Bowls and five conference championship games, but there was a growing sentiment that the window was closing on the Bill Belichick–Tom Brady era.

Soon after the Patriots' 2013 season ended in Denver in the AFC championship game against Peyton Manning and the Broncos, the Patriots went out and signed Pro Bowl cornerback Darrelle Revis to a two-year, $32 million contract. It was effectively a one-year rental of Revis's talents, because the first year was for an affordable $12 million, and the second year was a $20 million option. A day later, the Patriots signed another talented cornerback, Brandon Browner, to a three-year, $17 million contract.

On the offensive side of the ball, the Patriots signed free-agent wide receiver Brandon LaFell, and brought back restricted free agent Julian Edelman, who had enjoyed a breakout year as Tom Brady's favorite target in 2013 with 105 catches. And then in late August, just two weeks before the start of the

> Miami Dolphins linebacker Chris McCain (58) blocks a punt return by New England Patriots punter Ryan Allen (6) during the first half of an NFL preseason football game, in Miami Garden, Fla., Sunday Sept. 7, 2014. AP PHOTO/LYNNE SLADKY

regular season, the Patriots traded six-time Pro Bowl guard Logan Mankins to the Tampa Bay Buccaneers for tight end Tim Wright and a fourth-round pick in 2015. It was a stunning trade that saved the Patriots over 13 million real dollars over two years, and nearly $6 million in cap space for 2014. Wright had 54 catches as a rookie for the Bucs in 2013, and he could either be a complement or a replacement for Rob Gronkowski, who had missed 14 games the past two seasons due to injury, but Mankins was a nine-year veteran drafted by the Patriots in the first round, and a three-year captain. Belichick called him "one of the all-time great Patriots and the best guard (I) ever coached."

The Patriots, now ready to make a run at a fourth Super Bowl title in 14 years, began the season in Miami, and after they failed to get a first down on the year's first possession, Ryan Allen's punt was blocked. The Dolphins recovered at the Patriots' 15-yard line, and four plays later, Dolphin quarterback Ryan Tannehill threw a 4-yard touchdown pass to Lamar Miller. **The season was not off to a great start!**

The Patriots regrouped enough to take a 20–10 lead at halftime. Shane Vereen and Gronkowski scored touchdowns for the Patriots while the Dolphins committed three turnovers, but the second half was dominated by the Dolphins. They outscored the Patriots, 23–0, while the Patriots offense was held to just 67 yards. The Patriots lost their season opener for the first time since 2003, 33–20.

The Patriots gave up 191 rushing yards against the Dolphins, so they knew they had their work cut out for them in Week 2 when they'd be facing the Vikings and their All-Pro running back Adrian Peterson in Minnesota. But the Patriots never saw Peterson. The day before the game, he turned himself in to authorities in Montgomery County, Texas. Peterson was accused of spanking his four-year-old son with a switch, and had been indicted by a grand jury on charges of negligent injury to a child.

Without their star running back, the Vikings were held to just 54 yards rushing on 19 carries. Minnesota did, however, score on the game's opening drive when former Patriot quarterback Matt Cassell threw a 25-yard touchdown pass to Matt Asiata, but the Patriots' defense pitched a shutout from there. Along the way, they sacked Cassell six times and intercepted him four times. Devin McCourty had the first pick, and ran it back 60 yards all the way to the Vikings' 1-yard line, and Stevan Ridley ran it in from there to tie the score 7–7.

Revis's first interception as a Patriot also led to a touchdown—Brady throwing a 9-yard strike to Edelman to cap a 39-yard drive—but it was still a game when the Vikings lined up at the end of the first half for a field goal that could have cut the Patriots' lead to 17–10. Instead, Patriots defensive end **Chandler Jones blocked the field goal and ran it back 58 yards for a touchdown**, and the Patriots went up 24–7. A pair of second-half field goals by

Winningest Coaches

Bill Belichick now has 237 victories, which ranks him fourth all-time behind only Don Shula (328), George Halas (318) and Tom Landry (250).

> Minneapolis, Minn.: New England Patriots defensive end Chandler Jones (95) returns a blocked field goal for a touchdown during the second quarter against the Minnesota Vikings at TCF Bank Stadium. at TCF Bank Stadium, Sept. 14, 2014.
BRACE HEMMELGARN-USA TODAY SPORTS

Stephen Gostkowski accounted for the 30–7 final score, and Bill Belichick had his 200th career victory.

The Patriots were home for the third game of the season, and it was a surprisingly tough battle with the Oakland Raiders. The longest play of the game for either team was a 13-yard completion to Edelman. Brady improved to 57-5 in his last 62 home games, but was only able to lead the Patriots on one touchdown drive, finishing it off with a 6-yard throw to Gronkowski. A second chance to reach the end zone failed at the Raiders' 2-yard line when a low snap led to a hurried throw and an incompletion. The Patriots had to settle for one of their three field goals, and while they went on to win 16–9, it wasn't pretty.

"An ugly win is better than a pretty loss," Edelman would say.

The Raiders appeared to be marching toward a game-tying touchdown in the final minute of the game, but Darren McFadden's 6-yard touchdown run was called back due to a holding penalty. And on the very next play, Raiders rookie quarterback Derek Carr's pass went into the arms of his intended target Denarius Moore, but Rob Ninkovich knocked the ball away and Vince Wilfork came down with the third interception of his career. The Patriots ran out the clock and improved to 2-1.

The low point of the season happened at Arrowhead Stadium in Kansas City. The Patriots were humiliated by the Chiefs, 41–14. Tom Brady was strip sacked and was responsible for two interceptions, the second of which was returned 39 yards for a touchdown by Husain Abdullah, making the score 41–7. At that point, Brady was replaced by rookie quarterback Jimmy Garoppolo, who engineered an 81-yard drive and threw a 13-yard touchdown pass to Gronkowski. In his postgame interview, Bill Belichick was asked if the quarterback position would be evaluated. Belichick only smirked.

As bad as Brady and the offense were, and they were bad, the defense wasn't any better. The Chiefs had 303 yards of total offense in the first half alone. Already up 7–0 in the second quarter, the Chiefs raced down the field for 86 yards on three plays and took a 14–0 lead when Alex Smith connected on a 5-yard touchdown to Jamal Charles. It was one of three touchdown passes for Smith, and one of three touchdowns for Charles.

The worst sequence for the Patriots came at the start of the second half. On their first possession, they failed to get a first down and punted. On their second possession, Brady was sacked at his own 9-yard line and fumbled the ball away. The Chiefs scored two plays later. Brady was picked off on the second play of the ensuing possession, and that led to a Chiefs field goal that made it 27–0.

"We're on to Cincinnati," is what Belichick said five times at a news conference that week.

The Patriots were 2-2. They had won the AFC East five years in a row, and had been to the conference cham-

> Kansas City Chiefs free safety Husain Abdullah carries the ball after intercepting a pass and running it back 39 yards for a touchdown during the fourth quarter of an NFL football game against the New England Patriots, Monday, Sept. 29, 2014, in Kansas City, Mo. AP PHOTO/ED ZURGA

pionship game or beyond each of the past three seasons, yet they were already being written off in many corners of the NFL. For instance:

"It's becoming more and more apparent," wrote Steve DiMatteo of sbnation.com, "that Tom Brady is playing his age (he does age, and he's 37), and it might be time for you to reconfigure the way you think about Brady and the Patriots. Every great dynasty comes to an end eventually, and we could be witnessing the slow downfall of the NFL's dynasty of the new millennium."

In the week that followed there was an ESPN report that said Brady and the coaching staff were at odds with one another. Brady heard the noise, but went out and led the Patriots to a blowout victory over the Cincinnati Bengals.

"It's unfortunate that some things get said and talked about," Brady said, "especially when they don't come from me . . . I've got a lot of love and trust for everybody in this building. We all count on each other. We all rely on each other."

Despite all the questions swirling around their team all week, or perhaps because of them, the Patriots moved the ball easily on the game's opening drive. Brady completed passes to LaFell and Wright for a combined 70 yards, and Ridley capped the drive with a 1-yard touchdown run. The Patriots' second drive ended with a 27-yard pass to Gronkowski and a 17-yard → touchdown pass to Wright, and the Patriots led 14–0.

Cincinnati climbed back into the game in the third quarter when Adam Jones returned a punt 47 yards to the Patriots' 9-yard line, and Andy Dalton threw a touchdown pass on the next play to Mohamed Sanu. That cut the Patriots' lead to 20–10.

But Brady threw a 16-yard touchdown pass to Gronkowski to make it 27–10, and then the Bengals fumbled the ensuing kickoff. Brandon Bolden forced the fumble

› New England Patriots tight end Tim Wright (81) celebrates a touchdown in the game against the Cincinnati Bengals on Sunday October 5, 2014, at Gillette Stadium in Foxborough, Mass.
DAMIAN STROHMEYER AP IMAGES

> New England Patriots cornerback Kyle Arrington (25) tumbles into the end zone with a touchdown after recovering a fumble, as Cincinnati Bengals linebacker Marquis Flowers (53) defends in the second half of an NFL football game Sunday, Oct. 5, 2014, in Foxborough, Mass. AP PHOTO/STEVEN SENNE

and **Kyle Arrington scooped up the ball and ran it in from the 9**, and the Patriots were up 34–10. On the day, the Bengals lost three fumbles, and went 0-for-7 on third-down conversion attempts.

After losing in Kansas City, 41–14, the Patriots came home and beat the previously unbeaten Bengals, 43–17. It was quite the turnaround, and was the start of a seven-game winning streak in which the Patriots averaged 40 points per game, and had an average margin of victory of 20 points.

In Buffalo the next week, the Patriots got off to a slow start, but a pass interference call against the Bills in the end zone helped get the Patriots on the board. Following the penalty, Brady threw a 1-yard touchdown pass to Tim Wright. On the Bills' ensuing drive, Patriot linebacker Jerod Mayo injured his patellar tendon making a routine tackle on Bills running back Anthony Dixon. Mayo was carted off the field and lost for the season. The Patriots also lost running back Stevan Ridley to a knee injury in this game. Ridley's knee bent back awkwardly when he was tackled by Bills cornerback Stephon Gilmore in the third quarter. Ridley, the Patriots' lead running back with 94 carries and 340 yards to this point in the season, tore his ACL and MCL. **Both Ridley and Mayo were placed on season-ending injury reserve after the game.**

Meanwhile, a strip sack by Chandler Jones and a forced fumble by Devin McCourty led to a pair of Patriots field goals, and they took a 13–7 halftime lead.

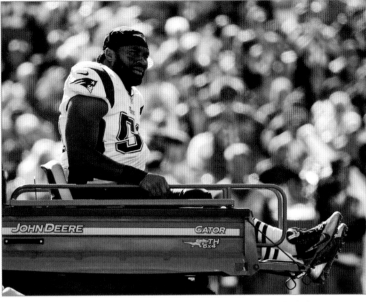

> New England Patriots middle linebacker Jerod Mayo (51) is carted off the field after being injured on a play during the first half of an NFL football game against the Buffalo Bills, Sunday, Oct. 12, 2014, in Orchard Park, N.Y. AP PHOTO/MIKE GROLL

> New England Patriots' Stevan Ridley (22) is slow to get up after being injured during the second half of an NFL football game against the Buffalo Bills Sunday, Oct. 12, 2014, in Orchard Park, N.Y. AP PHOTO/MIKE GROLL

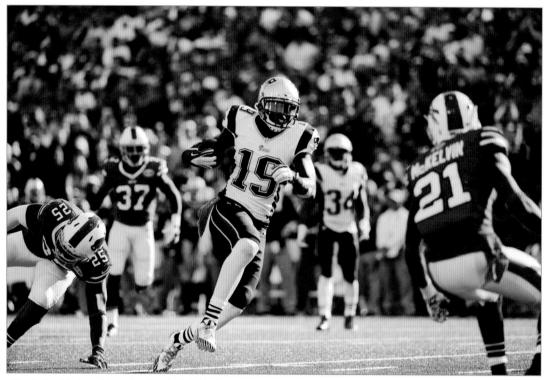

> New England Patriots wide receiver Brandon LaFell (19) runs for a touchdown against the Buffalo Bills during the second half of an NFL football game Sunday, Oct. 12, 2014, in Orchard Park, N.Y. AP PHOTO/MIKE GROLL

On the opening drive of the third quarter, Patriots wide receiver Brian Tyms split two Buffalo defenders, and Brady dropped a perfect pass into his arms from 43 yards away. Tyms caught the ball in stride as he fell into the end zone. And in the fourth quarter, **Brady threw 17- and 56-yard touchdown passes to LaFell**, and the Patriots rolled to a 37–22 win. Brady finished with four touchdown passes and 361 yards while improving his career record against the Bills to 23-2.

The Patriots were back home in Week 7 to face the 1-5 New York Jets. It took only 81 seconds for the Patriots to find the end zone. Brady stepped into a long throw to a streaking Shane Vereen, who snuck out of the backfield and sprinted down the sideline. **Vereen dove for the ball and barely got his hands under it as he landed on the goal line.** It looked like it might be an easy day for the Patriots, but the Jets used a power running attack to control the ball and the clock. They finished with over 40 minutes of ball possession and 218 yards rushing, and when Chris Ivory capped a 6:02 drive to open the third quarter with a 1-yard touchdown run, the Jets were in front 19–17.

> Oct 16, 2014; Foxborough, Mass.: New England Patriots running back Shane Vereen (34) catches the ball for a touchdown during the first half against the New York Jets at Gillette Stadium. MARK L. BAER/USA TODAY SPORTS

A Stephen Gostkowski field goal and a 3-yard touchdown pass to Vereen midway through the fourth quarter would put the Patriots back in control, but the Jets would not go down quietly. Geno Smith threw a 10-yard touchdown pass to Jeff Cumberland to make it a 27–25 Patriots lead with 2:31 to play. The Jets failed on the two-point conversion attempt that would have tied the game, but they forced the Patriots to punt on a three-and-out, and would still have a chance to win it. However, Patriots defensive tackle Chris Jones blocked a 58-yard field goal attempt as time expired. The Patriots had their third straight victory, and Brady had his 41st straight regular-season home victory against an AFC opponent—which is an insane stat!

After the battle with the Jets, the Patriots returned to blowing teams out, beginning with the Chicago Bears in Week 8. The game got completely out of hand during a 57-second sequence late in the first half. Brady threw a 2-yard touchdown pass to Gronkowski to put the Patriots ahead, 24–7, with under two minutes to go. The Bears ran three plays and punted, and Julian Edelman ran it back 42 yards. On the next play, Brady threw his fourth touchdown pass of

> New England Patriots defensive end Zach Moore (90) forces Chicago Bears quarterback Jay Cutler, center, to fumble in the first half of an NFL football game on Sunday, Oct. 26, 2014, in Foxborough, Mass. AP PHOTO/STEVEN SENNE

the first half—9 yards to LaFell. On the Bears' next play, **Zach Moore tomahawked the ball out of quarterback Jay Cutler's hands, and Rob Ninkovich picked up the fumble and ran it back for a touchdown.** Three touchdowns in less than a minute put the Patriots up, 38–7. Darrelle Revis intercepted Cutler on the final play of the half, and then Brady connected with Gronkowski on a 46-yard touchdown pass on the first drive of the third quarter. The Patriots rolled to a 51–23 win. In four consecutive wins, Brady had 14 touchdowns and no interceptions.

The Denver Broncos were next on the schedule, which meant another installment of Brady versus Peyton Manning, and for the 11th time in 16 matchups, Brady came out on top. Up 7–6 in

> New England Patriots wide receiver Julian Edelman (11) celebrates a touchdown catch from quarterback Tom Brady in the first half of an NFL football game against the Denver Broncos on Sunday, Nov. 2, 2014, in Foxborough, Mass. AP PHOTO/ELISE AMENDOLA

the second quarter, Manning was intercepted by Rob Ninkovich, who ran it back to the Broncos' 34. Four plays later, Brady threw a 5-yard touchdown pass to Edelman. The Broncos failed to get a first down on their next drive, and Edelman returned their punt 84 yards for a touchdown, and the rout was on!

"Minitron can do so many things," Brady said referring to Edelman. "He's so quick. What he did on the punt return was incredible."

What "Minitron" did was take a low line-drive kick from his own 16-yard line. He made the first man miss and sprinted to the right sideline, and when things got crowded over there, he cut back across the field, outrunning every Bronco to the left corner of the end zone. The Patriots led 20–7, and would make it 27–7 before halftime when Brady tossed a 5-yard touchdown strike to Vereen. Brady threw two more touchdown passes to LaFell and Gronkowski, and the Patriots ruled the day, 43–21!

> Indianapolis, Ind.: Patriots running back Jonas Gray (35) celebrates a first-half score against the Colts at Lucas Oil Stadium, Nov. 16, 2014. THOMAS J. RUSSO/USA TODAY SPORTS

After the bye week, **the Patriots surprised the Indianapolis Colts with a running back named Jonas Gray**. Signed off the practice squad when Ridley went down for the year, Gray had only 31 carries for 131 yards in his first three games as a pro, but against the Colts, he had 201 yards on 37 carries, and set a Patriot record with four rushing touchdowns. Where did that come from! And then where did he go? Gray was on the cover of *Sports Illustrated* two days after he steamrolled over the Colts and led the Patriots to a 42–20 victory. Three days after that, Gray overslept and was late for practice. That didn't go over well with Bill Belichick. So, when the Patriots lined up to play the Detroit Lions in Foxborough the following week, Gray didn't play at all. In fact, Gray was inactive for four of the Patriots' remaining nine games, including the Super Bowl.

The decision to bench Gray for the game against Detroit was made easier by **the return of LeGarrette Blount**. He had rushed for over 700 yards while with the Patriots in 2013, but signed with the Pittsburgh Steelers as an unrestricted free agent. The Steelers released him on November 18. The Patriots signed him on the 20th, and on the 23rd, he rushed for 78 yards and two touchdowns, and helped the Patriots beat Detroit, 34–9.

The first half was highlighted by **Danny Amendola's 81-yard kickoff return** that set up Blount's first touchdown of the day. Brady also threw a pair of first half touchdown passes to Tim Wright, and the Patriots took a 24–6 lead into halftime. To this point in the season, the Lions had given up the fewest points in the NFL, but the Patriots defense was the one that kept the opposition out of the end zone.

The Patriots' seven-game winning streak was snapped the next week in Green Bay. The Patriots had just one first down by the time the Packers had a pair of field goals and a 32-yard touchdown pass from Aaron Rodgers to Richard Rodgers. The Patriot offense finally came to life in the second quarter. Brandon Bolden

› New England Patriots running back LeGarrette Blount (29) runs from Detroit Lions strong safety James Ihedigbo (32) in the second half of an NFL football game Sunday, Nov. 23, 2014, in Foxborough, Mass. AP PHOTO/STEVEN SENNE

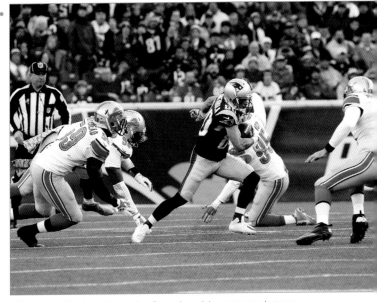

› New England Patriots wide receiver Danny Amendola, center, runs between Detroit Lions middle linebacker Tahir Whitehead, left, and long snapper Don Muhlbach (48) in the second half of an NFL football game Sunday, Nov. 23, 2014, in Foxborough, Mass. AP PHOTO/STEVEN SENNE

> New England Patriots quarterback Tom Brady is sacked by Green Bay Packers defensive end Mike Daniels during an NFL football game Sunday Nov. 30, 2014, in Green Bay, Wis. AP PHOTO/MATT LUDTKE

scored on a 6-yard run, and with 1:09 left in the first half LaFell caught a 2-yard touchdown pass from Brady to cut the Packers lead to 16–14. But the Packers only needed 55 seconds to go back up by nine points. Aaron Rodgers hit Jordy Nelson over the middle and he outraced Darrelle Revis and Devin McCourty to the end zone pylon. It was a 45-yard touchdown pass and a 23–14 Packer lead.

> New England Patriots wide receiver Julian Edelman (11) runs for a touchdown against the San Diego Chargers during the second half in an NFL football game Sunday, Dec. 7, 2014, in San Diego. AP PHOTO/DENIS POROY

The Patriots held the Packers to just a field goal in the second half, but a 15-yard touchdown pass from Brady to LaFell was all the offense could muster. It was 26–21 Green Bay when the Patriots moved the ball to the Packers' 20-yard line with three and a half minutes to play. **On third-and-9, Brady took a sack**, and then Stephen Gostkowski pushed a 47-yard field goal attempt wide right. It was the Patriots' last best chance to score, and they went on to lose, 26–21.

Instead of coming home after the game, the Patriots flew to the West Coast to prepare for their game against the Chargers. The decision to limit cross-country travel seemed like a good idea when the Patriots got back on the winning track. **A 69-yard touchdown pass to Edelman in the fourth quarter was the decisive play.** The Patriots won 23–14, and clinched their twelfth straight 10-win season.

The following week the Patriots were home against Miami and looking for revenge for the season-opening loss against the Dolphins, but on the game's first play from scrimmage, Dolphin wide receiver Mike Wallace beat a rookie cornerback named Malcolm Butler on a 50-yard pass

> New England Patriots strong safety Duron Harmon, right, runs back an interception as Miami Dolphins guard Mike Pouncey (51) gives chase in the first half of an NFL football game Sunday, Dec. 14, 2014, in Foxborough, Mass. AP PHOTO/STEVEN SENNE

play that put the Dolphins at the Patriots' 30-yard line. The Dolphins only gained seven more yards before attempting a 41-yard field goal, and the kick was blocked by Jamie Collins and returned by Kyle Arrington 62 yards for a touchdown!

In the second quarter, **Duron Harmon intercepted a Ryan Tannehill pass and took it back 60 yards** to the Miami 8-yard line, setting up a 3-yard touchdown run by Shane Vereen three plays later. It looked like the Patriots would take a 14–6 lead into halftime, but with 25 seconds to go in the half, the Patriots punted the ball away and Miami's Jarvis Landry ran it back 32 yards, and on the next play, Tannehill hit Wallace on a 32-yard touchdown pass that was initially called incomplete, but was reversed by instant replay.

In the third quarter the Patriots put up 24 points, which was a team record for the quarter. Blount had a short TD run. Patrick Chung had an interception. Gronkowski caught a 27-yard touchdown pass. And Julian Edelman scored on a 6-yard pass from Brady. Suddenly, what was a tough division game was a 41–13 division-clinching blowout.

> New York Jets kicker Nick Folk (2) watches as New England Patriots' Vince Wilfork (75) celebrates with teammates after Folk missed a field goal during the second half of an NFL football game Sunday, Dec. 21, 2014, in East Rutherford, N.J. AP PHOTO/BILL KOSTROUN

All that was left to do for the Patriots was to earn home-field advantage in the playoffs, and they did that with a 17–16 win over the Jets the following week. The Jets actually led 13–10 late in the third quarter, but Jets quarterback Geno Smith threw a floater intended for Jace Amaro that was an easy interception for Jamie Collins. The ensuing 38-yard drive concluded with Jonas Gray, back in Belichick's good graces and back on the field, scoring on a 1-yard run.

The Jets responded with a field goal to cut the Patriots lead to 17–16. Then midway through the fourth quarter, Brady's pass deflected off the hands of LaFell and into the hands of Marcus Williams, who made his first career interception. The Jets had the ball at the Patriots' 30-yard line—a golden opportunity to take the lead. Instead, Dont'a Hightower sacked Smith on third down and the Jets were forced to attempt a 52-yard field goal. Once again, just like they did in October, **the Patriots blocked Nick Folk's potential game-winning kick**. This time it was Vince Wilfork who got a hand on it. The Patriots ran out the clock from there and held on to win, 17–16. When the Broncos lost Monday night to the Bengals, the Patriots were assured of the number one seed in the AFC.

> New England Patriots wide receiver Danny Amendola, center, celebrates his 51-yard touchdown pass from Julian Edelman (11) in the second half of an NFL divisional playoff football game against the Baltimore Ravens Saturday, Jan. 10, 2015, in Foxborough, Mass.
AP PHOTO/ELISE AMENDOLA

Brady only played the first half of the season's final game against the Bills, and Gronkowski and Edelman didn't play at all. The Patriots lost for the first time at home in 16 games, and for the first time against an AFC opponent in 35 games—impressive streaks that mean nothing to the Patriots. Despite the 17–9 loss, the Patriots were ready for the playoffs!

After their well-earned bye week, the Patriots faced the Baltimore Ravens in the divisional round. Ravens quarterback Joe Flacco threw touchdown passes to Kamar Aiken and Steven Smith to give the Ravens their first 14-point lead. Brady, who holds every Patriot passing record, also tied Curtis Martin's playoff rushing touchdown record with his fifth in the final minute of the first quarter. He then threw a 15-yard touchdown pass to Danny Amendola to tie the game 14–14 in the second quarter. However, an uncharacteristic mistake by Brady put the Patriots in another hole. Brady threw an ill-advised pass that was intercepted by Daryl Smith with just over a minute to go in the half. The Ravens turned that into a 21–14 halftime lead when Flacco hit Owen Daniels with an 11-yard scoring pass with 10 seconds left in the half.

The Ravens had their second 14-point lead when Flacco and Justin Forsett connected on a 16-yard touchdown in the third quarter. And this is when things got a little weird. The Patriots ran a series of plays with only four offensive linemen, and running back Shane Vereen lined up outside the tackle box after he reported as an ineligible receiver. It was a strange formation that confused the Ravens. As they tried to figure out whom to cover, the Patriots converted short passes to tight end Michael Hoomanawanui and Edelman, and completed the drive with a 5-yard touchdown pass to Gronkowski.

Later, the Patriots tied the game 28–28 when Brady threw a pass to Edelman behind the line of scrimmage, and **the former Kent State quarterback fired a strike to Amendola, who was wide open and strolled into the end zone**. It was a 51-yard touchdown pass from one wide receiver to another!

The Patriots had erased a pair of 14-point deficits, but they still had work to do. After a Ravens field goal with 10 minutes to play, it appeared as though the Patriots had fumbled the game away. Vereen caught a 9-yard pass, but fumbled the ball and it was recovered by the Ravens. However, replays showed Vereen was down before he fumbled, and the Patriots' drive continued. It didn't end until Brady dropped a perfect pass over Rashaan Melvin's head right into the arms of LaFell streaking down the sideline and into the end zone. The Patriots had their

The Former Quarterback

In 31 games as quarterback of the Golden Flashes, Julian Edelman threw for 4,997 yards with 30 touchdowns and 31 interceptions. He only caught one pass for 11 yards.

> New England Patriots strong safety Duron Harmon (30) intercepts a pass by Baltimore Ravens quarterback Joe Flacco in front of Baltimore Ravens wide receiver Torrey Smith (82) in the second half of an NFL divisional playoff football game Saturday, Jan. 10, 2015, in Foxborough, Mass. AP PHOTO/CHARLES KRUPA

first lead of the game with just over five minutes to go. **Duron Harmon would intercept Flacco in the end zone**, Devin McCourty knocked down another pass into the end zone on the game's final play, and the Patriots advanced to the AFC championship game for the fourth straight year with a 35–31 win.

"It was a wild game," said Belichick, who tied Tom Landry for most postseason wins in NFL history with 20. "I'm just thankful our players hung in there and made the plays they needed to make."

In the AFC title game, the Patriots once again ran all over the Colts. Blount had run for 166 yards and four scores against the Colts in the divisional round of the 2013 playoffs. During the

> In this Jan. 18, 2015, file photo, New England Patriots tackle Nate Solder (77) makes a touchdown reception during the second half of the NFL football AFC Championship game against the Indianapolis Colts in Foxborough, Mass.
AP PHOTO/MATT SLOCUM

2014 regular season, it was Jonas Gray rushing for four touchdowns and 201 yards. And the Colts couldn't stop the Patriots running attack this time either. Blount had three touchdowns and 148 yards, and the Patriots won easily, 45–7.

The Patriots broke the game open in the third quarter when they scored touchdowns on all three of their possessions. **It started with a 16-yard pass from Brady to left tackle Nate Solder**, who was an eligible receiver on the play. Before the third quarter was over, Gronkowski and Blount also scored to make it 38–7, and then Blount scored again on the Patriots' first possession of the fourth quarter. The Patriots were headed back to the Super Bowl—but not without some controversy.

> In this Jan. 18, 2015, file photo, New England Patriots quarterback Tom Brady has a ball tossed to him during warmups before the NFL football AFC Championship game against the Indianapolis Colts in Foxborough, Mass.
AP PHOTO/MATT SLOCUM

The AFC championship game will forever be remembered as the game that launched "Deflategate." On first-and-10 at the Colts, 26-yard line in the first quarter, Brady's pass was intercepted by D'Qwell Jackson. He brought the ball to the sideline where the Colts' equipment manager got hold of it and told Colts head coach Chuck Pagano the ball seemed a bit under inflated. Word got out to Colts general manager Ryan Grigson, who called the NFL's director of field operations. What followed was nearly two years of investigations, intrigue, court battles, and ultimately, a four-game suspension for Brady. But while controversy swirled, the Patriots added two more Lombardi Trophies to their collection.

The first one, or rather the Patriots' fourth one, was earned in Glendale, Arizona, on February 1, 2015. Despite two weeks' worth of Deflategate questions, the Patriots kept their focus on the task at hand and outlasted the Seattle Seahawks in one of the best Super Bowls ever played.

The game did not start well for the Patriots. On their second possession, Brady brought the Patriots to the Seattle 10-yard line, but then threw a pass that floated into the arms of Seattle's Jeremy Lane, who was standing on the goal line. Seattle couldn't do anything with the ball and punted it away. The Patriots went right back to work and moved the ball 65 yards on nine plays. Brandon LaFell's 11-yard touchdown reception accounted for the game's first points.

The teams traded touchdowns by Marshawn Lynch and Rob Gronkowski. So, the Patriots led 14–7 when the Seahawks got the ball at their own 20 with 31 seconds to go in the first half. Seattle began with a 19-yard run by Robert Turbin, followed by a 17-yard scramble by quarterback Russell Wilson. A 23-yard pass from Wilson to Ricardo Lockette got the ball to the Patriots, 11-yard line with six seconds to go in the half. There was time for one quick throw into the end zone, and the Seahawks pulled it off. Wilson found unlikely contributor Chris Matthews in the left corner of the end zone and the game was tied 14–14. Matthews, by the way, was a rookie who didn't have a catch during the regular season, but he'd have four catches for 109 yards in the Super Bowl.

The vaunted Seattle defense took over in the third quarter, intercepting Brady for a second time, and holding the Patriots to just one first down in the quarter. Meanwhile, the Seahawks kicked a field goal and added a touchdown pass to Doug Baldwin to take a 24–14 lead.

The Patriot offense came to life in the fourth quarter. Brady found Edelman on a pair of 21-yard passes, and then Brady hit Amendola in the end zone. The Patriots trailed 24–21 with just under eight minutes to play. After the Patriot defense forced a three-and-out, Brady marched the Patriots 64 yards for the go-ahead score, a 3-yard pass to Edelman.

Seattle got the ball with 2:02 left in the game, and trailing 28–24. A beautiful pass along the sideline from Wilson to Lynch picked up 31 yards and brought the game to the two-minute

> Seahawks wide receiver Jermaine Kearse (15) makes a 33-yard catch during the second half of NFL Super Bowl XLIX football game against the New England Patriots Sunday, Feb. 1, 2015, in Glendale, Ariz. AP PHOTO/DAVID J. PHILLIP

warning. **Another deep ball, this time to the other sideline to Jevon Kearse**, picked up another 33 yards and put the ball at the Patriots' 5-yard line. There was still 1:06 on the clock, and the Seahawks were 15 feet away from victory. Lynch rushed for four yards on first down, and he was expected by many to get the ball on second down, but the Seahawks

> New England Patriots strong safety Malcolm Butler (21) intercepts a pass intended for Seattle Seahawks wide receiver Ricardo Lockette (83) during the second half of NFL Super Bowl XLIX football game Sunday, Feb. 1, 2015, in Glendale, Ariz. AP PHOTO/KATHY WILLENS

opted for the element of surprise. They threw the ball! **Wilson's pass was intercepted by Malcolm Butler**, and the Patriots were Super Bowl champions once again!

"I've been at it for 15 years," Brady said, "and we've had a couple of tough losses in this game. This one came down to the end, and this time we made the plays."

Yup, cue the duck boats! New England's got another one!

CHAPTER TEN

THE
2016 NEW ENGLAND PATRIOTS

Owner:
Robert Kraft

Director of Player Personnel:
Nick Caserio

Head Coach:
Bill Belichick

Regular Season Record:
14-2

Regular Season Finish:
AFC East Champions

Playoff Results:
Divisional Round—New England Patriots 34
Houston Texans 16

AFC Championship—New England Patriots 36
Pittsburgh Steelers 17

Super Bowl:
New England Patriots 34, Atlanta Falcons 28
(OT)

Awards:
Super Bowl MVP: QB Tom Brady

Pro Bowlers: QB Tom Brady, LB Dont'a
Hightower, S Devin McCourty,
SpT Matthew Slater

With 10 championships in 15 years, it may seem as though Boston sports fans have enjoyed one, long consistent euphoric ride. Not so. There have been a couple of last-place finishes by the Red Sox. The Celtics had to hit rock bottom before winning their 17th banner. The Bruins have missed the playoffs several times along the way. And the 2015 New England Patriots provided plenty of disappointment and confusion. Twice when they had a chance to clinch home-field advantage throughout the playoffs, they blew it! Pushed into overtime by the New York Jets in Week 16, the Patriots won the coin toss, but elected to kick the ball away. The Jets' Eric Decker beat Malcolm Butler for a touchdown, and the Patriots lost. The following week, the Patriots rested and protected their starters, and lost at the Miami Dolphins. So, when it came time to play the AFC championship game, the Patriots traveled to Denver. In that game, Bill Belichick opted twice to go for first downs instead of kicking short field goals, and Stephen Gostkowski missed an extra point for the first time in 524 tries. With those seven points squandered, the Patriots had to go for a two-point conversion with 12 seconds left. Tom Brady's pass intended for

> Colorado Rockies' Daniel Descalso (3) stands on deck as fans unfurl a "Free Brady" sign referring to New England Patriots quarterback Tom Brady and the "Deflategate" controversy during a baseball game at Fenway Park, Thursday, May 26, 2016, in Boston. AP PHOTO/ELISE AMENDOLA

Rob Gronkowski was intercepted by Denver's Bradley Roby, and the Patriots lost 20–18.

After an offseason in which the Patriots' Pro Bowl linebacker Jerod Mayo retired, Pro Bowl defensive end Chandler Jones was traded to the Arizona Cardinals, and wide receiver Brandon LaFell was released, the **Patriots began the 2016 season with Tom Brady serving a four-game suspension for his alleged involvement in Deflategate**.

The Patriots began the season in Arizona with quarterback Jimmy Garoppolo making his first NFL start. **Garoppolo got the year started with a 37-yard touchdown pass to Chris Hogan on the Patriots' opening drive**. Hogan was a four-year lacrosse player at Penn State, and only played one year of football at Monmouth University. He wasn't

> New England Patriots quarterback Jimmy Garoppolo (10) makes a call against the Arizona Cardinals during an NFL football game, Sunday, Sept. 11, 2016, in Glendale, Ariz. AP PHOTO/ROSS D. FRANKLIN

drafted, but played three years with the Buffalo Bills before the Patriots signed him as a free agent in March 2016.

The Patriots added a field goal and were up 10–0 when Garoppolo was sacked by Markus Golden and fumbled the ball, which was recovered by former teammate Chandler Jones. The Cardinals marched 54 yards and scored on a 3-yard touchdown pass from Carson Palmer to Larry Fitzgerald, cutting the Patriots' lead to 10–7 at the half.

The Patriots opened the second half with an 8-yard touchdown run by LeGarrette Blount, but Blount fumbled the ball away on the Patriots' next possession, and the Cardinals again converted the turnover into points. David Johnson's 1-yard touchdown run cut the Patriots' lead to 17–14.

Midway through the fourth quarter, another short touchdown pass to Fitzgerald gave the Cardinals a 21–20 lead. Garoppolo then did what Brady had done so many times before. He led the Patriots on a game-winning drive. Faced with a third-and-15 from his own 20, Garoppolo found Danny Amendola for a 32-yard pickup and a crucial first down. The drive would eventually sputter,

➤ Miami Dolphins linebacker Kiko Alonso, right, hits New England Patriots quarterback Jimmy Garoppolo (10) after he threw a pass during the first half of an NFL football game Sunday, Sept. 18, 2016, in Foxborough, Mass. Garoppolo was injured on the play and did not return to the game. AP PHOTO/STEW MILNE

but Gostkowski kicked a 32-yard go-ahead field goal with 3:44 to go.

The game came down to a 47-yard field goal attempt by Arizona's Chandler Catanzaro, and he missed it! With a backup quarterback making his first NFL start, and playing on the road against a team considered to be a Super Bowl contender, and with Rob Gronkowski sidelined by a hamstring injury, the Patriots still came away with a 23–21 win.

"I am really proud of our team tonight," Belichick said. "I thought we got great effort from all three phases. We played a good complementary game."

Garoppolo followed his impressive first NFL start by throwing touchdown passes on each of the Patriots' first three drives against the Miami Dolphins. He threw for 234 yards in the first half and led the Patriots to a 21–0 lead, but with less than five minutes to go in the half, **Garoppolo was tackled by Miami linebacker Kiko Alonso**. Garoppolo landed hard on his throwing shoulder with the weight of Alonso driving him into the ground. The result was a Grade 2 AC joint injury, and Garoppolo was done for the day. In fact, Garoppolo wouldn't take another meaningful snap all year.

> New England Patriots running back LeGarrette Blount runs for a touchdown during a NFL football game against the Miami Dolphins at Gillette Stadium in Foxborough, Mass. Sunday, Sept. 18, 2016. WINSLOW TOWNSON/AP IMAGES FOR PANINI

It was up to rookie quarterback Jacoby Brissett to finish the game. Brissett was taken in the third round of the 2016 draft, and he handled himself quite well in his first NFL action. He opened the second half with a short pass to Martellus Bennett. Bennett, who was acquired during the offseason in a trade with the Chicago Bears, took the ball 37 yards up the left sideline. Blount finished the drive with a 9-yard touchdown run to give the Patriots a 31–3 lead. Even with a third-string quarterback pressed into action, the game was secure. The Patriots would give up a pair of fourth quarter touchdowns, but improved to 2-0 with a 31–17 victory. Brissett was 6-for-9 for 92 yards. **Blount ran for 123 yards**, and Bennett had five catches for 114 yards.

Garoppolo wasn't available to play in Week 3, so Brissett made his first NFL start at home against the Houston Texans, who were nice enough to turn the ball over three times, twice on kickoff returns to set up Patriot touchdowns. In the first quarter, Brandon Bolden forced Houston's Charles James to fumble, and Duron Harmon recovered the ball at the Texans' 27-yard line. James was initially ruled down by contact, but Bill Belichick challenged the call, and it was reversed. **On the very next play, Brissett faked a handoff, rolled to his right, and raced down the sideline for a 27-yard touchdown run.**

Following a Patriot field goal in the third quarter, Stephen Gostkowski kicked off to Houston's Tyler Ervin. Nate Ebner forced the fumble and recovered the ball at Houston's 21-yard line. Six plays later, Blount rushed in from the 1, and the Patriots led 20–0. Blount capped off the game's scoring with an exciting 41-yard dash to the end zone in the fourth quarter. Blount broke a tackle behind the line of scrimmage, hit the hole, and outraced a slew of Houston defenders. The Patriots won 27–0. It was their first shutout in four years, and they were 3-0 with just one more game to play without Tom Brady.

That game was against the Buffalo Bills, and it would be the first time the Patriots were ever shutout at Gillette Stadium. Brissett got the start, and only managed 13 first downs. The Bills, meanwhile,

> New England Patriots quarterback Jacoby Brissett (7) dives into the end zone for a touchdown past Houston Texans linebacker Max Bullough (53) during the first half of an NFL football game Thursday, Sept. 22, 2016, in Foxborough, Mass. AP PHOTO/CHARLES KRUPA

scored on their opening drive when Tyrod Taylor threw a 7-yard touchdown pass to LeSean McCoy. Three Buffalo field goals were the only other points put on the board, and the Patriots lost 16–0.

"God, it feels good to finally win here," Bills coach Rex Ryan said. "It's satisfying, but let's face it, they had a player out."

That player, of course, was Tom Brady, and his suspension was now over. The Patriots played the first four games of the season without the best quarterback on the planet, and with the best tight end, Rob Gronkowski, catching just one pass for 11 yards, and they were still 3-1. It was time to get the season started!

The Patriots were in Cleveland for Week 5, and Tom Brady returned with an eight-play, 80-yard drive that included a 34-yard catch and rumble by Gronkowski, and concluded with a 1-yard touchdown run by Blount. The next time the Patriots touched the ball they went 75 yards on eight plays and again found the end zone when Brady hit Martellus Bennett from 7 yards away. The Patriots would make it three straight scoring drives when Brady threw a 43-yard bomb to Chris Hogan, who made a diving catch inside the 10, and three plays later, Brady found Bennett again for a 5-yard touchdown. Brady and Bennett would connect a third time on a 37-yard touchdown to open the second half. **Brady's comeback included 406 yards passing—114 of them to Hogan, another 109 to Gronkowski—three touchdowns to Bennett, and a 33–13 victory!** ⎯⎯⎯⎯•

Getting Shut Out at Home

The Patriots have only been shutout at home nine times in their history. The last time they were shutout in Foxborough was a 6-0 loss to the New York Jets on November 28, 1993.

➤ Oct 9, 2016; Cleveland, Ohio; New England Patriots quarterback Tom Brady (12) and tight end Martellus Bennett (88) celebrate a touchdown during the first quarter against the Cleveland Browns at FirstEnergy Stadium. KEN BLAZE-USA TODAY SPORTS

"This isn't a time for me to reflect," Brady said. "There's no point at looking back at anything. Whether we won Super Bowls or lost championship games, or the last four weeks, none of it matters. I've just moved on, man."

Brady's first home game of the 2016 season was against the Bengals. He and the Patriots got off to a bit of a slow start, but with a minute to go in the first half, Brady hit James White out of the backfield with a pass that White caught at the Bengals, 10-yard line, and ran it in from there. The Patriots led, 10–7.

The Bengals opened the second half with a touchdown pass from Andy Dalton to Brandon LaFell to take a 14–10 lead. When the Patriots had to punt on their next possession, it seemed like the momentum had shifted, **but Dont'a Hightower sacked Dalton in the end zone for a safety, and the Patriots took off from there**.

A 38-yard pass to Gronkowski on the Patriots' next possession put the ball at the Bengals'

➤ New England Patriots linebacker Dont'a Hightower, left, sacks Cincinnati Bengals quarterback Andy Dalton for a safety during the second half of an NFL football game, Sunday, Oct. 16, 2016, in Foxborough, Mass. AP PHOTO/STEVEN SENNE

> New England Patriots tight end Rob Gronkowski (87) celebrates a touchdown by spiking the ball during the 2016 NFL week 6 football game against the Cincinnati Bengals on Sunday, Oct. 16, 2016, in Foxborough, Mass. The Patriots defeated the Bengals 35-17. JIM MAHONEY VIA AP

> New England Patriots tight end Rob Gronkowski winds up to spike the ball after catching a touchdown pass against the Cincinnati Bengals during the second half of an NFL football game, Sunday, Oct. 16, 2016, in Foxborough, Mass. AP PHOTO/ELISE AMENDOLA

4-yard line, and **Gronk caught the touchdown pass on the next play**. The Bengals went three-and-out, and Brady hit Gronk for another 38-yard pickup. That was Brady's 5,000th completion, and three plays later, White ran it in from the 4. Gostkowski missed the extra point, but the Patriots had scored 15 points in a little over four minutes, and took a 25–14 lead. They went on to win, 35–17. Brady finished with 376 yards passing, and three more touchdown passes. Gronk had one of those touchdowns and a career-high 162 yards receiving.

The following week the Patriots were in Pittsburgh to face the Steelers without quarterback Ben Roethlisberger, out with a torn meniscus in his left knee. His replacement, Landry Jones, was intercepted by Malcolm Butler in the first quarter, and the Patriots scored on the ensuing drive on a 19-yard pass from Brady to White to take a 7–0 lead.

The Patriots scored on their next possession when Blount ran in from the 3, but the Steelers came back with 13 unanswered points to make it a 14–13 Patriots lead midway through the third

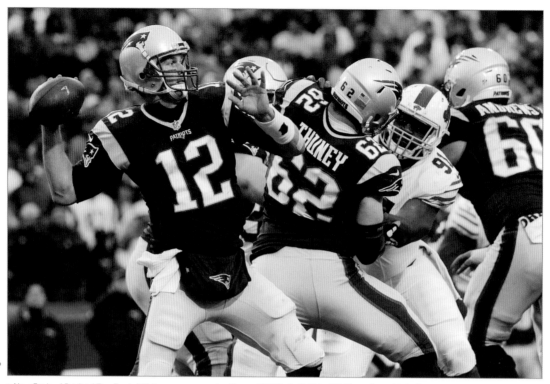

> New England Patriots' Tom Brady (12) throws a pass as Joe Thuney (62) blocks Buffalo Bills' Leger Douzable (91) during the second half of an NFL football game Sunday, Oct. 30, 2016, in Orchard Park, N.Y. AP PHOTO/ADRIAN KRAUS

quarter. The Patriots needed a big drive, and they got it! Blount ran for 11 and 25 yards, and Brady put a perfect pass into the hands of Gronkowski running down the seam for a 36-yard touchdown. The Steelers responded with a field goal before the Patriots came up with another touchdown drive. Gronkowski picked up another 37 yards and Blount scored on a 5-yard run, and the Patriots went on to win, 27–16.

If anyone was having trouble quantifying Tom Brady's impact, it became crystal clear in Week 8 when the Patriots traveled to Buffalo. **Without Brady in Week 4, the Patriots were shutout. With Brady in Week 8, the Patriots scored 41 points**. Can you say difference maker?

In the first half, Brady threw a 9-yard touchdown pass to Danny Amendola, and a pair of 53-yard touchdowns to Hogan and Gronkowski. The first quarter pass to Hogan was perhaps the highest pass Brady has ever thrown—a rainbow that fell into Hogan's arms at the 10, and he trotted in from there. The second quarter pass to Gronkowski was over the middle, and Gronk outraced the defender the final 25 yards and danced into the end zone. It was Gronkowski's franchise-record 69th career touchdown.

> New England Patriots' Danny Amendola (80) returns a kickoff during the second half of an NFL football game against the Buffalo Bills Sunday, Oct. 30, 2016, in Orchard Park, N.Y. AP PHOTO/BILL WIPPERT

The Patriots opened up the second half with **a 73-yard kickoff return by Amendola. He was spun around at midfield and finally taken down from behind at the Bills' 24**. Brady threw a pair of 12-yard passes, first to Bennett and then to Julian Edelman to give the Patriots a 31–10 lead. It was another 315 yards and four touchdowns passing for Brady, and a 41–25 win. The Patriots were 7-1 and headed into the bye week.

Bill Belichick, never timid when it comes to personnel moves, made the bold decision on the first day of the bye week to trade his Pro Bowl linebacker Jamie Collins to the Cleveland Browns for a compensatory third-round pick. It was a sudden and surprising move, because Collins was considered one of the Patriots' best and most athletic defenders, but the Patriots had already reduced his role because of a perceived weakness against the run. The Patriots had also prepared for this move when they acquired linebacker Kyle Van Noy from the Detroit Lions five days earlier.

So, the Patriots, who had the third-ranked defense in the NFL in points allowed, moved forward, and in their first game without Collins, they allowed 31 points and 420 total yards in a loss to the Seattle Seahawks. The Patriots opened the game with a drive that included a 22-yard pass to Gronkowski. It was the Patriots' 252nd consecutive pass without an interception, a new NFL record for the start of the season. The drive ended with a 1-yard touchdown run by LeGarrette Blount, and the Patriots took a 7–0 lead.

The Patriots failed to get a first down on their next two possessions, and were finally intercepted on the next one. DeShawn Shead made the pick. By then, the Seahawks had kicked two field goals and scored on a Russell Wilson to Doug Baldwin 6-yard touchdown. Shea McClellin blocked the extra point, so the Patriots trailed 12–7. In the second quarter, Gronkowski took an especially hard hit from Seahawks safety Earl Thomas and temporarily left the game. The drive continued, however, and Blount again rushed in from the 1, and the Patriots were back in front 14–12 with just over a minute to play in the first half. That was enough time for the Seahawks! Wilson tossed a deep ball to a wide-open Doug Baldwin in the right side of the end zone, and Seattle took a 19–14 halftime lead.

Blount ran for a third touchdown in the third quarter, but the Patriots found themselves behind 25–24 midway through the fourth quarter. Brady completed a pass over the middle to Edelman, but the ball was ripped free by Kam Chancellor and recovered by Richard Sherman. The Seahawks converted the turnover into a third touchdown pass to Baldwin. In an effort to make it a two-score game, the Seahawks went for the two-point conversion leading 31–24. This time a pass to Baldwin fell to the ground, and the Patriots would have a chance to tie or even win it.

They got the ball with over four minutes left and proceeded to march down the field. The big plays were a 30-yard reception by Edelman on a third-and-10, and a 26-yarder to Gronkowski that gave the Patriots first-and-goal from the two. Brady tried twice to run it in, but couldn't. Blount tried once, and was stopped. **So, on fourth down, Brady looked for Gronkowski on a fade route to the right side. There was a lot of contact between Gronk and Chancellor, but no flag on the play. The Patriots lost, 31–24.** It was the last time the Patriots would lose all year. They ran off seven straight wins to end the regular season, and then, of course, won three playoff games, including their fifth Super Bowl.

The winning streak started with Tom Brady returning to the Bay Area to play his first game on San Francisco's home field. Having grown up in nearby San Mateo, it was a homecoming for Brady, and he celebrated it with four touchdown passes and a 33–17 victory.

"It was very cool," he said. "It doesn't get any better than that. To have the first chance to ever do that was very special. I felt it in pregame warmup and it carried right to the last play of the game. It was pretty great."

> New England Patriots tight end Rob Gronkowski (87) can't catch a pass in the end zone over Seattle Seahawks safety Kam Chancellor (31) in the final moments of an NFL football game, Sunday, Nov. 13, 2016, in Foxborough, Mass. The Seahawks defeated the Patriots 31–24.
MATT WEST/THE BOSTON HERALD VIA AP

Brady's first touchdown pass was a 4-yarder to Edelman, who managed to get his feet in bounds while making the catch in the end zone, but Gostkowski missed another extra point, and the Patriots led 6–0. Brady's next touchdown pass was a 9-yarder to James White in the second quarter to give the Patriots a 13–3 lead. It was still anybody's game deep into the third quarter when Brady threw a 5-yard touchdown pass to Amendola to put the Patriots ahead, 20–10. And Brady sealed the deal when he avoided a rush and fired a strike to rookie wide receiver Malcolm Mitchell, who hauled in the pass and outraced the Niners' defense for a 56-yard touchdown. Brady had won his 199th game, tied for second most all-time with Brett Favre, and one behind Peyton Manning for first place.

Brady would move into a tie for the top spot the following week in the Meadowlands against the New York Jets. Gronkowski, who had missed the Niners game with a chest injury, was knocked out of the Jets game late in the first quarter with a back injury. The Patriots were trailing 10–0 at the time, and were struggling to move the ball. They managed a 28-yard field goal by Gostkowski, and then turned the tide when Malcolm Butler stripped the ball away from Robby Anderson and recovered it at the 50-yard line. The Patriots scored on the ensuing drive when Brady picked up a fumbled snap and threw a 4-yard touchdown pass to Mitchell. The game was tied and far from over. Before halftime, Alan Branch blocked a 54-yard field goal attempt by the Jets' Nick Folk, and Gostkowski sent a 39-yard field goal attempt wide left.

The Patriots took a 13–10 lead to the fourth quarter, but the Jets' Quincy Enunwa brought down a 22-yard pass from Ryan Fitzpatrick in the back of the end zone. Enunwa didn't get both feet down, but his backside landed in the end zone. So, while the play was initially ruled an incomplete pass, the call was reversed by replay. The Jets led 17–13, but managed just one first down the rest of the way. Meanwhile, the Patriots kicked a field goal and later got the ball back with just over five minutes to play. Brady completed 24- and 25-yard passes to Edelman and Hogan, and completed the game-winning drive with an 8-yard touchdown pass to Mitchell. The two-point conversion failed, but the Patriots led 22–17 with just under two minutes to play. The Jets had time, but soon they didn't have the ball! Chris Long sacked Fitzpatrick, forcing a fumble recovered by Trey Flowers, and the Patriots were 9-2!

But the news wasn't all good. Days later, it was announced that Gronkowski would undergo surgery for a herniated disc in his back. He was done for the season. Again, the Patriots simply moved on.

Tom Brady's record-breaking 201st career victory began like so many of his victories before: with an opening drive touchdown. But this one was unlike any other. This time, on fourth-and-1, LeGarrette Blount bounced a run to the outside, made Rams safety Maurice Alexander trip over himself, and sprinted 43 yards down the right sideline for his 13th touchdown of the year. **Following an → interception by Malcolm Butler, Brady threw a 14-yard touchdown pass to Hogan.** Gostkowski kicked four field goals and the Patriots won again, 26–10.

> New England Patriots cornerback Malcolm Butler celebrates his interception against the Los Angeles Rams during the first half of an NFL football game, Sunday, Dec. 4, 2016, in Foxborough, Mass.
AP PHOTO/STEVEN SENNE

"It's always been about winning," Brady said about his 201st win. "I've been very fortunate to be on a lot of great teams. I'm just really grateful."

The next Monday night against the Ravens, Brady, who was already without Gronkowski, would also be without Danny Amendola, who suffered a high ankle sprain against the Rams. Undeterred, Brady threw for 406 yards and three touchdowns against the NFL's top-ranked defense. It was the Patriots' defense that actually got on the board first. After punter Ryan Allen's punt was downed at the 1, Malcolm Butler tackled Kenneth Dixon in the end zone for the Patriots' third safety of the year—a franchise record. **Still in the first quarter and after Shea McClellin leaped over the snapper to block a field goal,** the Patriots went 74 yards on 10 plays and scored on a Blount 1-yard rush.

On the Patriots' next possession, Brady threw a 9-yard pass to James White, who caught it on the right side and ran diagonally down the field for a 61-yard pickup. Brady would throw a 6-yard touchdown pass to Mitchell, giving the Patriots a 16–0 lead.

> New England Patriots linebacker Shea McClellin (58) blocks a field goal attempt by Baltimore Ravens kicker Justin Tucker, partially hidden behind Patriots' Jonathan Jones (31), during the first half of an NFL football game, Monday, Dec. 12, 2016, in Foxborough, Mass.
AP PHOTO/STEVEN SENNE

In the second half, the Patriots used a perfectly executed flea flicker to pick up 28 yards on their way to another touchdown. Brady handed the ball off to Blount, who ran a few steps before turning around and flipping the ball back to Brady, who hit Chris Hogan in stride. Hogan was ankle-tackled at the 24, and Brady would eventually find Bennett in the end zone. Bennett outmuscled the Ravens' Zachary Moore and the Patriots had a 23–3 lead.

That's when the trouble started! The Patriots turned the ball over on back-to-back special teams plays. First, Cyrus Jones had a punt brush against his foot, and the Ravens recovered at the Patriots 3. From there, Joe Flacco threw a touchdown pass to Darren Waller. Then, on the ensuing kickoff, Matt Slater was hit and fumbled, and the Ravens again recovered deep in Patriot territory. Flacco's 8-yard touchdown pass to Kenneth Dixon cut the Patriots lead to 23–17.

Late in the fourth quarter, the Ravens drove to the Patriots' 12, but were forced to kick a field goal when Rob Ninkovich sacked Flacco. Now, it was 23–20, but not for long. On the Patriots' first play from scrimmage, the Ravens lined up without a body on Chris Hogan. He sprinted up the seam and Brady lobbed him a perfect pass. The 79-yard touchdown was the 450th of Brady's career. The Patriots went on to win, 30–23.

A few days after the game, the Patriots made the curious move of signing wide receiver Michael Floyd, who had just been released by the Arizona Cardinals following a drunk driving arrest. Floyd gave the Patriots depth at the position and insurance in case Amendola was unable to play again that season.

Next up for the Patriots was a trip to Denver, where they had lost the AFC championship game the year before, and where Tom Brady had a 3-6 career record. Brady did not have a great game, but his defense did. The Patriots held the Broncos to a first quarter field goal and went on to win, 16–3, clinching their record eighth consecutive division title.

It was a 3–3 game late in the first quarter when Broncos quarterback Trevor Siemian led a drive to the Patriots' 14, but was intercepted by Logan Ryan. The Patriots took over on their own 8, and Brady was immediately strip sacked by Jared Crick, but offensive lineman Joe Thuney pounced on the ball, and the drive continued. Later, running back Dion Lewis recovered his own fumble inside the Denver 5, and again the drive continued. LeGarrette Blount finished the drive with his 15th rushing touchdown, establishing a new single-season Patriot record.

It was a defensive struggle with both teams punting seven times, but the Patriots' defense won the day, and what was quickly developing into a championship defense went out the following week and forced the New York Jets to turn the ball over four times.

Malcolm Butler had three of the turnovers. In the first quarter, he intercepted Bryce Petty at the Jets' 47-yard line, and that led to a 5-yard touchdown pass from Brady to Martellus Bennett and a 10–0 lead. In the second quarter, rookie linebacker Elandon Roberts knocked the ball out of Khiry Robinson's hands, and Butler jumped on the fumble. That led to a field goal. And in the third quarter, Butler picked off Ryan Fitzpatrick, setting up another Blount short touchdown run. His 17th TD of the season gave the Patriots a 41–0 lead. It was the turnovers that made all the difference. The Patriots only had 325 total yards in the beatdown, but they played on a short field all day, and Brady finished with three touchdown passes to Bennett, James White, and tight end Matt Lengel—who made his first NFL reception. Brady sat out the entire fourth quarter, and the Patriots rolled to a 41–3 win.

In the final game of the regular season, the Patriots played at Miami knowing that a win would clinch the top seed in the Eastern Conference. So, they played all out! They dominated the Dolphins and finished the regular season undefeated on the road.

The game started with a 2-yard touchdown pass to Bennett on the opening drive. The Patriots forced a three-and-out, and then Brady threw his first-ever touchdown pass to Michael Floyd. It was the 65th different receiver who had caught a touchdown pass from Brady. Two field goals by Stephen Gostkowski gave the Patriots a 20–0 lead before the Dolphins found the end zone on an 8-yard connection from Matt Moore to Jarvis Landry.

The Dolphins also scored on the opening possession of the third quarter when a fumble recovery by Butler was nullified by a penalty, and then Moore found a wide-open Kenny Stills in the end zone for a 22-yard touchdown. Stills had easily slipped behind linebacker Kyle Van Noy, but as Belichick explained in a conference call the next day, it wasn't Van Noy's fault.

Most Super Bowl Appearances

With their ninth Super Bowl appearance in franchise history, the Patriots now hold the record all by themselves. The Dallas Cowboys, Denver Broncos, and Pittsburgh Steelers have all appeared in eight Super Bowls.

"The players were trying to do the right thing," he said. "They had the right idea. We were trying to apply something, and we just didn't have it right. And that really goes back to me more than anybody else, so I'll take that one."

Suddenly, it was a 20–14 game, but not for long. On the Patriots' next drive, **Brady hit Edelman on a short pass to the left side. Three defenders converged, but Edelman split them all and began racing down the field. Just as Dolphins defensive back Tony Lippett was about to reach him, Michael Floyd appeared and delivered a devastating block. Lippett went tumbling to the ground,** and Edelman went 77 yards for the longest reception of his career.

> New England Patriots wide receiver Michael Floyd (14) throws a big block on Miami Dolphins cornerback Tony Lippett (36) during the NFL week 17 football game on Sunday, Jan. 1, 2017, in Miami Gardens, Fla. The Patriots defeated the Dolphins 35–14. JIM MAHONEY VIA AP

The victory wasn't secure just yet. Trailing 27–14, the Dolphins brought the ball inside the Patriots' 10 with over eight minutes to play. Moore threw a short pass to Damien Williams, who was quickly corralled by Devin McCourty. The ball popped free and Shea McClellin scooped it up. He ran 69 yards before he was finally hauled down at the Dolphins' 18. When Blount rushed in from the one, and then ran in from the two for the two-point conversion, the victory was secured. The Patriots finished the season with a 35–14 win and a 14-2 record. Brady finished his abridged season with 28 touchdown passes and two interceptions, which was the highest TD/INT ratio in league history. The Patriots were ready to begin another Super Bowl run!

After their bye week, the Patriots hosted the Houston Texans, the same team they had smoked 27–0 behind a third-string quarterback during the regular season, but the Texans came into Gillette Stadium with the NFL's top-ranked defense, and it showed. Brady, who threw just two interceptions in 12 regular-season games, had two passes picked off by the Texans. Brady also threw a 13-yard touchdown pass to Dion Lewis in the first quarter to give the Patriots a 7–0 lead. Then, following a

> New England Patriots running back Dion Lewis (33) runs past Houston Texans linebacker Benardrick McKinney (55) for a touchdown during the first half of an NFL divisional playoff football game, Saturday, Jan. 14, 2017, in Foxborough, Mass. AP PHOTO/STEVEN SENNE

Texans field goal, **Lewis caught the kickoff at the 2, broke an ankle-tackle at the 30, and outraced the entire Texans special teams unit down the right sideline. It was a 98-yard kickoff return for a touchdown and a 14–3 Patriot lead!**

Houston rallied back with the help of their first interception, which bounced off the hands of Michael Floyd and into the arms of A. J. Bouye. That led to a 27-yard field goal. And this time on the ensuing kickoff, Lewis took a hit from Akeem Dent and fumbled the ball away. Eddie Pleasant recovered at the Patriots' 12, and the Texans later scored on an 8-yard touchdown pass from Brock Osweiler to C. J. Fiedorowicz. Now it was a 14–13 Patriot lead.

The Patriots made it 24–13 in the third quarter when Brady lofted a 19-yard touchdown pass over the head of Benardrick McKinney that found James White in the right corner of the end zone. Later, Lewis added a 1-yard touchdown run, making him the first player in the Super Bowl era to score on a

On Mental Toughness

We won a lot of different ways under a lot of different circumstances," Brady said in the postgame press conference. "Mental toughness is what it is all about and this team has got it. We'll see if we can write the perfect ending.❞

catch, a kick return, and a rush in a postseason game. In between the White and Lewis touchdowns, the Patriots picked off Osweiler twice, and they'd get him a third time before the game was over. The Patriots advanced to a record sixth straight conference title game with a 34–16 win. Belichick and Brady were going to their 11th conference championship game together. No other head coach and quarterback tandem have been to more than six.

And with a surprisingly easy 36–17 win in the AFC title game over the Pittsburgh Steelers, who had won nine games in a row, the Patriots won their ninth consecutive game and advanced to the Super Bowl for the seventh time under the ownership of Robert Kraft and the leadership of Belichick and Brady.

Chris Hogan was the star of this one. He caught a 16-yard touchdown pass in the first quarter, and then was on the receiving end of another Patriots flea flicker. This time Brady's handoff went to Dion Lewis, who pitched it back to Brady, and Hogan was wide open for the 34-yard touchdown that gave the Patriots a 17–6 lead.

A third quarter touchdown drive included a 39-yard pass to Hogan, who would finish the day with nine catches for 180 yards. The drive also included an 18-yard run by Blount, who carried a large portion of the Steelers defense with him to the 1-yard line. Blount ran it in for the touchdown from there and the Patriots led, 27–9. Kyle Van Noy forced a fumble on the Steelers' next drive and recovered the ball on the Steelers' 28. Four plays later, Julian Edelman caught a 10-yard touchdown pass from Brady, who finished with 384 yards and three touchdown passes.

The Patriots faced the high-flying Atlanta Falcons at NRG Stadium in Houston, Texas, in Super Bowl LI, and if the perfect ending is a 25-point comeback, redemption, and revenge for Deflategate, and an unprecedented fifth Super Bowl for both Belichick and Brady, then the Patriots did, in fact, write the perfect ending. Of course, there's no comeback possible unless the Patriots first dig themselves into a giant hole, and they began shoveling when LeGarrette Blount fumbled early in the second quarter. That led to the game's first points when the Falcons put together a 71-yard drive, and Devonta Freeman ran in from the 5. After a Patriots punt, Falcon quarterback Matt Ryan threw a 19-yard touchdown pass to Austin Hooper, and it was 14–0.

With the help of three defensive holding penalties, the Patriots moved the ball to the Falcons' 23. It looked like the Patriots were about to start digging out of the hole. Instead it got deeper. Brady threw short left toward Amendola, but two defenders stepped in front of him. Falcon cornerback Robert Alford picked off the pass and ran 82 yards for the pick-six and a 21–0 lead with 2:21 left in the first half.

The Patriots managed a 41-yard field goal before Lady Gaga came out to perform the halftime show, and then things got worse. The Falcons extended their lead. Matt Ryan threw a 6-yard strike to Tevin Coleman to make it 28–3 midway through the third quarter. The 25-point hole was complete. No team had ever come back from more than 10 points down in a Super Bowl, but the Patriots were about to score on five consecutive drives while their defense shutout the Falcons the rest of the way.

The comeback began with the Patriots facing fourth-and-3 at their own 46. They had to go for it! Brady found Amendola, who made the catch and carried it to the Falcons' 37, a gain of 17 yards and a much-needed first down. Three plays later, facing a third down and 8, Brady went back to pass, but rolled out of the pocket to his right, and scrambled 15 yards for another huge first down. The drive ended with a 5-yard touchdown pass from Brady to James White, but Stephen Gostkowski missed the extra point, so the score was 28–9.

Kyle Van Noy and Trey Flowers converged to sack Ryan on the Falcons' ensuing drive, and the Patriots drove for more points. They got all the way to the Falcons' 10, but Brady was sacked by Grady Jarrett, and the Patriots had to settle for a 33-yard Gostkowski field goal. That made it a two-score game, as long as the Patriots could score two touchdowns and two two-point conversions.

This is where the magic started to happen! Dont'a Hightower came off the left edge and ran unimpeded until he slammed into Ryan and forced a fumble that Alan Branch recovered at the Falcons' 25-yard line.

"Hightower's turnover was the key play," Belichick would say later. "Without that I don't know if we have enough possessions, or can get it done quickly enough."

Brady was immediately sacked, but converted a third-and-11 with a 12-yard pass to rookie receiver Malcolm Mitchell. Amendola caught a 6-yard touchdown pass, and James White ran through the line for the two-point conversion, and suddenly it was 28–20 with just under six minutes to play. There was still time, but if Atlanta scored, the game would effectively be over.

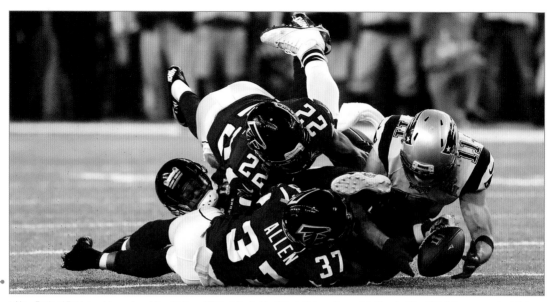

> New England Patriots wide receiver Julian Edelman (11) is defended by Atlanta Falcons free safety Ricardo Allen (37), Falcons cornerback Robert Alford (23), and Falcons rookie strong safety Keanu Neal (22) as Edelman makes a diving circus catch with the ball inches off the turf on a pass reception good for a gain of 23 yards and a first down at the Falcons' 41-yard line on a key fourth quarter drive with two minutes left in regulation play during the Super Bowl LI football game against the Atlanta Falcons on Sunday, Feb. 5, 2017 in Houston. The Patriots won the game 34–28 in overtime. PAUL SPINELLI VIA AP

Hearts sank in New England when Matt Ryan avoided the rush and threw a perfect pass just over the fingertips of Eric Rowe and Julio Jones made a sensational leaping catch, landing on his left foot and tapping his right foot in bounds for a 27-yard pickup. The Falcons had a first down at the Patriot 22. They were well within field goal range. However, after a 1-yard loss on a Freeman rush, Trey Flowers bull-rushed up the middle and sacked Ryan at the 35-yard line. Now, the Falcons were barely in field goal range, and an offensive holding call on Jake Matthews on the next play would push the ball back another 10 yards. The Falcons were forced to punt, and the Patriots took over at their 9 with 3:30 to play.

The game-tying drive included one of the greatest catches in Super Bowl history. Julian Edelman was the intended target, but Robert Alford got a hand on the ball, and deflected it high into the air. Alford fell to the ground, but Edelman stopped on a dime and dove back toward the ball. Before it hit the ground, the ball bounced off Alford's shin, giving Edelman just enough room to get his hands under the ball and make the catch.

"I got it! I caught it!" Edelman shouted while still on the ground.

And he was right. The play was upheld on review, and the Patriots' drive continued. They still had 41 yards to go, and they picked those up on a 20-yard pass to Amendola, two completions to

> New England Patriots' James White scores the winning touchdown between Atlanta Falcons' Jalen Collins, left, and Robert Alford during overtime of the NFL Super Bowl LI football game Sunday, Feb. 5, 2017, in Houston. AP PHOTO/ELISE AMENDOLA

James White for 20 yards, and a 1-yard rushing touchdown by White with under a minute to go in regulation. The Patriots added the two-point conversion on a bubble screen pass to Amendola, tying the game 28–28, and for the first time in history, the Super Bowl was going to overtime!

The Patriots correctly called heads and took the ball. A touchdown would win it. Brady completed five consecutive passes to four different receivers to get the ball to Atlanta's 25. White ran for 10, and a pass interference call against De'Vondre Campbell put the ball on the 2. **James White ran it in from there and the Patriots had done what seemed like the impossible.** They scored 31 unanswered points and won Super Bowl LI in overtime, 34–28!

Count the rings! That's 10!

"A lot has transpired over the last two years," Robert Kraft would say to the crowd in Houston with confetti falling down all around him. "And I don't think that needs any explanation. But I want to say to our fans, our brilliant coaching staff, our amazing players, who are so spectacular: This is unequivocally the sweetest."

ABOUT THE AUTHOR

Bob Halloran is a Boston-based award winning journalist, accomplished author, movie consultant, and sports-writer. Currently the sports anchor for Boston's ABC affiliate, WCVB, his broadcast career has included roles at ESPN, WFXT in Boston, and WPRI in Providence, Rhode Island. At ESPN, Bob spent three years as an anchor and writer for ESPN. com. Halloran has written several books, including *Irish Thunder: The Hard Life and Times of Micky Ward* and *Impact Statement: A Family's Fight for Justice Against Whitey Bulger, Stephen Flemmi and the FBI.* Halloran has won a New England Emmy Award for sportscasting and two honors from the Associated Press. He lives in the Boston area.

> PHOTO GRETJE FERGUSON